FROM MIDDLE CLASS
TO MILLIONAIRE
YOU CAN DO IT

KATHRYN M. CRAIG

ACKNOWLEDGEMENTS

I'd like to thank my husband who supported me in every way as I wrote this book. Thank you husband.

I'd like to thank my beautiful little princess for her love. She also tried to help me by typing, editing, and getting the pages as they printed.

I'd like to thank my parents. Thanks to my family.

I'd like to thank Amazon.com and Createspace.com which made all of this possible and easy to do.

I thank Jesus most importantly for the inspiration and desire to write. I also need to thank him for the motivation to finish this instead of giving up. Thank you Lord.

TABLE OF CONTENTS

CHAPTER ONE

SOMETHING TO PONDER

Why do you work? To survive may be your answer. Yes. That's true. Most of us are not in debt because we're trying to survive though. We're in debt because we overextend ourselves trying to establish and maintain an image. If we were working just to survive, many of us would not have the type of debt we have.

Regardless of whether you work to survive or to maintain an image, I know you are tired of working hard and living paycheck to paycheck. Wouldn't it be nice to not have to live this way? How about not having to be stressed by working a job you don't like because you have to pay your bills? There is more than one solution to help you avoid getting massive amounts of debt. If you already have lots of debt, in this book I'll give you several plans to help you get rid of it.

This book is not going to teach you how to make money with a pyramid scheme. It's not a get rich quick scheme. You don't have to sell anything. It's a book to help your everyday average middle class person who goes to work forty hours a week for fifty weeks out of the year get out of debt and amass a small fortune over time.

It's going to teach you how to arrange your money to pay your bills. You won't become a millionaire overnight. It's a process that occurs over time. You can become a millionaire. You don't have to eat a worm in the jungle while you outwit, outplay, and outlast in Survivor. You don't have to be smarter than a fifth grader. You don't have to hit the lotto. You do not have to have a college degree to follow this plan or to become a millionaire.

You should be able to get your hair and nails done, or go and buy yourself a cup of coffee for four dollars everyday if you like or whatever you want. You work hard. You deserve it. In order to do this and be debt free, you may have to make some sacrifices for a few years; that's all. Wouldn't you prefer to have to sacrifice financially for a few years instead of feeling like you're struggling for the rest of your life? I would.

CHAPTER TWO

THINGS TO BE CONSIDERED

TAXES: There is no legal way to avoid paying taxes. Besides, we like the benefits taxes allow us to enjoy. I always tell myself to not begrudge paying the price for anything I enjoy. I enjoy having paved roads, lit streets, mail delivery for six days, and so many other things that are provided by taxes. Get over having to pay taxes or go to jail.

FICA: You might as well get over this one too. Most of us do not know what FICA is and why we have to contribute to it, but we do.

SOCIAL SECURITY: This is the one deduction I hate paying. We're paying into the Social Security system. If you're younger than a baby boomer, you're being told you will never withdraw any of the money you're paying into this system. I heard President George W. Bush, while he was in office say in an interview that this money isn't used for Social Security payments. So why are we paying our hard earned money into this black hole? So we don't go to jail. Also, we cannot elect to stop the payments.

The theory is, there will be so many baby boomers withdrawing money from the Social Security System there will not be enough funds for the generations following them. My question is, if so many of them will be withdrawing money from the system, what about the amounts of money they should have been paying into the system. There should be stockpiles of money waiting on them. There benefits should not depend on my contributions. I know noone really knows the answers. The money we contribute is being stolen and wasted away in a system of corruption. I don't know what we can do about it. If you have any suggestions, write your congressmen.

MEDICARE: is another deduction you're doling your money out to without knowing if you're ever benefit from it.

COST OF LIVING: this will affect your timing of getting your million, but the calculations themselves will not change. What I mean by cost of living is where you live and the cost you may have to pay to live there varies in different areas of the country. The cost of a home in Alabama will be drastically different than purchasing one in certain areas of New York. A million is a million regardless.

BONUSES, COMMISSIONS, OVERTIME, AND RAISES: These will all affect how fast or slow you achieve your goal. Work hard to achieve your goal.

INSURANCE: it is very important to get insurance on your cars, homes, and most importantly, yourself. You may not understand the importance of insurance, but it doesn't mean you shouldn't get it. Trust me, when you need it, you'll learn and understand the importance really fast. I will advise you to pay for your insurance six months to a year in advance when you can. The reason: if you pay month by month, five dollars or more is added to your payment for processing. That's another sixty dollars or more you can use toward wealth building for yourself, not the insurance company.

TITHES AND OFFERINGS: The main difference in this book and many others is many financial advisors will advise you to pay yourself at least ten percent of your salary first. If they don't suggest you pay yourself first, they will tell you to donate to a charity.

I am suggesting to you to pay your tithe first, which means ten percent of your salary to your church first. Don't forget to include your offering. You may be thinking this is the whole point of this book. I'm going to slyly try to convert you. We Americans act like we are so against giving this advice because we may offend someone else. I cannot convince you to convert any more than the IN GOD WE TRUST that's printed on each piece of money you spend. If the benefits of spending your money with God's name imprinted on it is not enough to convict you, who am I? Every time you write or acknowledge what year it is, you're showing conviction whether you want to or not.

VACATIONS: when you begin working, do allocate time to take vacations and personal days. I know it would seem as if I would not have to tell you to do this. I needed someone to tell me because I was stupidly working, working, working. I was working so hard after I graduated from college, I didn't think to take vacations. I was so accustomed to vacations being scheduled for me, I didn't think about it. The result of my not taking vacation time resulted in me being sick and having to take a week or so off work anyway. Your body is going to make you take a break whether you want to or not. So, I'm making sure I tell anyone who needs to know.

Follow the plan, which includes taking time off to relax. You will get paid so it's not like you're being a louse. Do not take extravagant trips if you're drowning in debt. I shouldn't have to tell you this. I will just in case you act like you don't know.

CHAPTER THREE

SUGGESTIONS TO SUCCEED USING THE PLAN

These suggestions are things you will do temporarily to help you accomplish a goal. For instance, if you were paying for a house and/or a car, you would want to do these things to help you accomplish your goal so you won't become overwhelmed with debt. They are not things you will have to do for your entire life. Life is for living. You must enjoy it. There are times when you have to make sacrifices also.

1. The best way to succeed in the plan is to be aggressive. What I mean by being aggressive is to pay your basic survival bills and your minimum payments on your credit cards. You will set aside some money for Murphy's Law situations. The rest of your money will be used to make bulk payments on your mortgage and/or car.

2. If you're being aggressive with the plan, which I suggest you do, you will not have cable. You can have a cell phone, because some people do not use landlines. You will not text or buy all these different ring tones for the phone until you get where you want to with your money.

You can keep yourself busy by doing all of the things you said you would do if you had more time. You can spend more time with your family and friends. I have more suggestions in the book.

3. If you want to be a stay at home mom, this plan will be

great so you won't have to worry about finances if everything is paid off. This is why I suggest waiting until the plan is working before having children. It may only take three years if you're aggressive. It will also depend on your goals.

4. You may choose not to tell your friends that you are participating in the plan until you have bought your first home. Some people aren't very supportive when you are trying to do something positive like this for your life. It's not that they don't like you or want the best for you. Most people do not realize they can live better than their mediocre lives of living from paycheck to paycheck. I received a lot of negative comments when I would tell people I was trying to pay all of my bills off. I was told that I would always have bills so I should just get over that. I was told that I would always have utilities to pay if nothing more. I latter heard in interview on the radio where this guy said he paid his utilities by six months to a year in advance. Wow! I thought that's the way I could get away from having to think about those bills. You can have your utilities automatically deducted from your account nowadays.

I would also get comments from people saying they wouldn't think I had financial problems. I feel like having any debt is a financial problem. I do not like having any bills. I hate the month to month having to take time out for paying bills. I prefer to pay cash for purchases so I can avoid it. For most of the things that we are buying for our day-to-day consumption, which we are in debt for, it really isn't as big an expense as the debt we carry.

I want to further explain this thought. I lot of the credit card debt we carry isn't for needs. The emergency we experience that has caused our debt accumulation is an event where we believe we need a new outfit to wear. We overlook all the other unused garments in our closets. We're getting in debt because we have to buy items that are on sale and we couldn't possibly leave it in the store.

5. One of the biggest problems you may find in following this plan is not being able to eat out all the time. You will have to stop being lazy or not taking time out to plan your day. You can prepare your grits or oatmeal in the morning. If that's too difficult you can make a simple bowl of cereal. You can make your own cup of coffee. I can assure you if you're willing to sacrifice this for a little while, you will be able to eat out as much as you may like without worry about a bill. I know if you don't sacrifice now, you will be charging these simple meals on your credit card and you will be carrying a balance on it for eternity.

You can also make a sandwich or have leftovers from your previous nights meal for lunch. Cup-o-Noodles will be a great meal. The point is, you can buy groceries to help reduce your debt load. Dinner may be the only meal that will take some time and effort, but it doesn't have to be with all the prepared meals available at the grocery store.

I know there will be times when you did not properly prepare for the next day. We have all been there. It happens. Grab some fruit you've bought. I was going to suggest you buy an inexpensive lunch, but I know too many of you would use this excuse to buy lunch everyday. Plus inexpensive is relative. What I may consider as inexpensive, like a kid's meal, you may go to a place with fine dining.

6. There are times when you do need to spend a little money on yourself to make life enjoyable. I believe you should always buy yourself a nice gift on your birthday. I do not wait for others to acknowledge my birthday. It's fun when other people do, but I will never be disappointed if someone doesn't get me what I consider to be a great birthday present, Valentine's gift, or Christmas present. Yes, I have had people laugh at me because I do this. If you want flowers, don't wait on someone to get them for you, get them yourself

and don't be ashamed to say, "I bought myself some flowers." Life is too short not to get simple things you want sometimes.

7. Probably the most important thing you may need to change your thinking about to be successful with the plan is the way you feel about your job. A lot of us absolutely do not like our jobs. Your job is what will help you be successful. If you need help appreciating your job more, think of it as you've hit the lotto that will be paid over a lifetime. Others will receive lump sum payments. Or think of it as the source of the gift you receive every month, every two weeks, or whenever it is that you receive your paycheck. Some of us would complain about our job even if it was an at home job where we printed the money we needed to pay for our needs. There's no making some of us happy.

The funny thing about the job we have is we actually made the effort to apply for this job. Most of us do not have the luxury of having an employer scouting us. How and why many of us dislike our jobs is not the subject matter of discussion here. The advice I can give you is go to work and do your best. When you've actualized enough of the plan where you're able to move to your next adventure, move on.

CHAPTER FOUR

BUYING A CAR

Purchasing a car will probably be the first major financial investment a person makes. In the scheme of things, most people don't look at a car purchase as an investment. The reason it's not looked at as an investment is because it looses value instead of gaining. When it is getting you to and fro the place you are investing your time to get money to ensure your survival, it's an investment.

Your first car purchase probably should not be a new car unless you're willing to make sacrifices until you're able to buy it outright. The reason I'm emphasizing outright, paid in full purchases on a house and car is because these items will take up the bulk of your money earned. They will cause you to live paycheck to paycheck if you let the balances linger year after year.

If you're willing, you can sacrifice getting a new car as your first new car purchase. Get something that is reliable and can get you from point a to b. It should be inexpensive enough for you to pay off in one payment or within a few months of saving. This is advice for someone just starting out.

If you are drowning in debt, you shouldn't be trying to buy a car anyway. Hopefully you're not in need of a car. If you are, follow the advice of someone just getting started.

If you have money that's eating a hole in your pocket and you're not just starting out, I suggest saving all the money you need to purchase the car you want, and negotiating a better price because you can when you're paying in full.

I believe everyone who can afford to get a new car should have a new car. There's nothing like it. The new car smell is mesmerizing. The knowledge that you're putting its first miles on it is a great feeling.

The time for purchasing your new car will depend on your goals. If you want to purchase a home, you should save for and purchase your home first. Then, after your home is paid for, you should save for your new car purchase.

The mistake that is made too often is people will buy a house and a car at the same time or within a few years of each other. These large payments will cause your paychecks to become maximized.

If you have already financed your car and you're making payments, make more than the minimum payments. You can pay your car off early and avoid paying a lot of interest. I paid my car off in two years. It can be done.

CHAPTER FIVE

THE BIGGEST MISTAKE WHEN BUYING A HOME

When you are purchasing a home, the first thing the Real Estate agent will tell you to do is get a pre-approval amount from the bank. Yes, they want you to get this pre-approval so you won't waste their time. Most agents will not want to be bothered with you without the bank's pre-approval. Who can count how many times they have gone house shopping to find out the person isn't eligible to get a house. Yet, this isn't the biggest mistake.

The biggest mistake when purchasing a home is to believe you have to use all of the money the bank says you are pre-approved to buy your house. The bank will give you this astronomical figure. They do not give you a figure in the middle of the pendulum's swing. They do not necessarily consider how much your insurance will be. They are not considering if you will have to pay for trash pick-up, fire dues, or association fees. They do not know how much your groceries cost each month or what other information you may be including or leaving out so you can get pre- approved for the greatest amount. There are some things you have to know and be aware of for yourself. Yes. You do want to get the greatest amount of money for your pre-approval. This will allow you to get as much house as you're willing to work for and clean. You do not have to feel obligated to use every cent. You probably should not use every cent. You have to consider the things you like to do besides working for your mortgage payment.

Some things you will need to think about when looking for a home is upkeep. Is it going to be too large for you and your family? There can be such a thing. What I mean by this is not only will you visit each room daily, but also are you going to be willing to keep it clean, or hire someone to help you keep it clean. You can have more toilets in a house than you have butts to put on them. They will still need to be cleaned. I know all of your closets will be used so I don't have to address that one. For some people the kitchen will never get used, but I've never seen a house that did not come with one so consider it as a buy a house, get a kitchen free deal. It's just the way it is.

If you have a yard, you have to groom it yourself or hire a landscaper. You have to have money for all the maintenance because you are responsible. Some people find this as a valid reason to continue to live in an apartment. I disagree because you do not have to get a very large yard. You can reduce your maintenance woes by scheduling services in certain months at certain times of the month. You will have your money ready for payment after it's done. Voila!

CHAPTER SIX

THE SECOND BIGGEST HOME BUYING MISTAKE

The second biggest mistake made when buying a home is you have to pay your mortgage an entire thirty years before it becomes yours. Believe it or not, you can pay your home off before fifteen or thirty years. This is what I've realized. How can this be?

If you are willing to pay for a prestige automobile and pay it off in approximately five years, why wouldn't you be able to buy a home in that amount of time? There is no reason.

What happens to most of us is we spread our paychecks too thin. A home is the largest purchase we will make. We mortgage the home, new automobiles and furniture all within the same month. We'll buy a home then, we think we need a new car to go with the new home. Of course you have to get new furnishing, bedding, dishes, and clothes. By this time, your paycheck is maximized.

This is why I advise to save for your home instead of mortgaging it. If you can alleviate the practice of accumulating so much debt all at once, your life will be easier.

CHAPTER SEVEN

THE THIRD BIGGEST HOME BUYING MISTAKE

Adjusted Rate Mortgages (ARM) loans are the biggest scam next to credit cards if you don't use them correctly. I know a person would sign for an ARM loan if it were giving an unusually low interest rate. Most people who get ARM loans do not know what they are signing for or why. They don't know that when the loan adjusts they should try to reapply for another loan with a better rate. It can be a big mess. It can cause some people to loose their homes because they cannot afford the payments on the adjusted loan. You have to know these things for yourself. A banker will sell you on this because their concern is making money.

CHAPTER EIGHT

SIMPLE CALCULATIONS

When I say simple calculations, I really literally mean these calculations are simple. They are so simple you are probably thinking, Kathryn, I don't need you to tell me how to calculate a million dollars. If you don't have a million dollars these simple calculations may help you see clearer how you can get it.

I'm going to work with simple calculations because there's no need to work with anything else. When you file your taxes, the IRS has you round everything off to the nearest whole dollar. We're going to work in that way of thought. If your life's numbers are more complicated, round them to the nearest whole dollar.

It's predicted that most of us will have to work until age seventy. If you want, you can work the projected fifty years and earn twenty thousand dollars a year to become a millionaire. The reason I included the THINGS TO BE CONSIDERED chapter is we all know taxes and deductions will be taken out to run the government. You can make the adjustments for that by making more money. You also know that there are people who make less than twenty thousand dollars a year and those who make more than a hundred thousand dollars a year. Make the necessary adjustments for your income.

$$20,000 \times 50 \text{ years} = 1,000,000$$
$$50,000 \times 20 \text{ years} = 1,000,000$$
$$100,000 \times 10 \text{ years} = 1,000,000$$

If you want to make a million dollars and be able to see it and enjoy it in your lifetime, there are several things you'll need to do. I will give several scenarios. Pick the one that closest fits your lifestyle.

CHAPTER NINE

IF YOU'RE JUST GETTING STARTED

If you're twenty and you're just getting started with your life, this is going to be a great plan for you to live a lifestyle of luxury without some stressors. You can attain this lifestyle whether you have or haven't graduated from high school or college. Success with this plan is determined by how willing you are to work to accomplish it.

In this scenario we'll have you still living at home with your parents. If you decide to move into an apartment, it will take money away from the plan. Many of you will feel you cannot live with your parents. You're an adult and they want you to follow their rules, like having a curfew. It will be so beneficial to you to bite the bullet and stay with them. Help out around the house. If you have to pay a bill or some rent to stay with them, do it. I know you're not going to pay them the money, but you can help keep the house clean and cook a meal. It's going to help you out so much in the long run.

If you tell them you are trying to save money so you can move out, they may not bother you about paying any bills. I think after some time of saving, you should pay them something. Nothing in life is free. They're paying the bills so you don't have to, but you're taking away from their abilities to see their million dollars sooner.

You'll need to get a job or two jobs where you will be making at least twenty thousand dollars a year. This plan will work for anyone starting out with any amount of money. We will discuss the twenty thousand dollars a year amount.

Twenty thousand dollars a year divided by fifty-two weeks in a year equals three hundred and eighty-five dollars a week you'll need to earn. You will need to work forty hours a week, which means you will have to earn a minimum of nine dollars and sixty-two cents an hour to make it. This is the lowest you can make on the fifty- year plan, so anything you make over this amount will get you to where you want faster. Okay, now that didn't take any fancy footwork.

If you or your parents haven't bought you a car, you need to buy a jalopy as soon as possible. You need it to get you to and fro work. You do not need it to get you to the beach unless that's where you work. If you live in an area where it's not practical to have a car, skip this part and move on to the next goal.

You will save the money from your first month's check to get yourself a used car. You will also need to get car insurance. Most states if not all, will require you to get liability insurance. This is enough insurance to cover the other person if you're in an accident. It does not cover your vehicle. If you bought a jalopy, it doesn't make any sense to have more than that anyway. The insurance is not going to cover getting your vehicle repaired anyway. You will be wasting money to pay for any additional coverage.

You'll also have to set aside some money to buy gas and for maintenance each time you get paid. What you'll be doing with all of your money is saving it anyway, but you should keep money for gas on you because some banks charge fees if you access your account over a certain amount of times each month.

If you have friends who want to go out all the time, you'll have to decide not to if you want to achieve your goal. Occasionally, you should go out. Everyone needs a break sometimes to get away from the monotony. There is going to come a time when you will be able to go out and spend your money like you want. Now is just not the time. It won't take a long time, but it will take time. You will have to be patient. You and all of your friends are probably struggling financially right now. If you follow the plan, you won't be broke for long.

What you will have to remember is the deductions taken out of your check from the THINGS TO BE CONSIDERED chapter. You will not make exactly twenty thousand dollars because of them. You will have to determine how to reduce your expenses to the bare minimum. You will also need to decide if you will work extra to make more money, or find a job that pays more money. This may mean you'll have to forego some working hours for education. The great thing about going to college is you don't have to be there all day every day. Either way if you want this plan to work, it will be easier if you put off having children for a few years.

While you are working and saving your money, you can start looking at houses you may want to buy. If you are making twenty thousand dollars a year, you are not going to be able to afford a three hundred thousand dollar home. Depending on your circumstance, the bank will pre-approve you for at least three times your salary. Normally you have to get pre-approved when you want to look at homes. That time will come. What you're going to be doing now is looking at neighborhoods you want to live in and types of homes you like. This is going to help you with your goal setting. It'll let you know for what you need to strive. You're saving your money so you can buy your house outright. I know I know. Everything you've heard about buying a house has been to pay a mortgage over a thirty- year period, fifteen at the least. You are not going to do it that way. You're going to look for a home that you can pay off in approximately two to three years. You're going to save your money. You're going to work hard for the next two to three years, while continuing to live at home with your parents. Your expenses will almost be nonexistent because you are trying to achieve your goal. You can do this. You will be glad you did this when you have achieved your goal.

You may have to move into a starter home. That's fine. This will be better than paying rent. If you were to decide to move into an apartment, you would be helping someone else become a millionaire. When you move into your own house, you will be giving yourself a great gift. Even if you were to have to pay a mortgage every month, you are still investing in yourself, so it's not a bad deal. You don't want to do the paying a mortgage thing though. You don't have to do it. So don't do it.

I did mention cost of living in THE THINGS TO BE CONSIDERED section. Another thing that has to be considered in cost of living is the area of the country you live in. Some people live in areas where homes are very expensive. You will have to sacrifice longer. Trust me it won't kill you.

I have done and am still doing some of this plan. It is a lifestyle plan which means it will be something you will be able to use throughout your life to avoid debt. It's a process. It's not as difficult to accomplish as you may think. You may think you don't want to spend time doing this plan. You're young and you want to spend your money shopping and partying. Well, you can do that with all of your money and stay broke. Time will pass and you will be broke. You can choose to follow this financial plan, have something to show for your money as time passes.

The sooner you start; the better off you'll be in the long run. If you're having doubts about the plan, just try it and see how good it will make you feel knowing you have money to get the things you want and need without having to use credit cards or going in debt. The added benefit is you get to enjoy your money while you're young and not have to wait until you retire.

After you have saved the money to get into your home. It will take about three years of strict saving to get it if you move into a house around fifty to sixty thousand dollars. You can possibly negotiate a better deal on the house being you will pay in full.

When you move in, the relief you will have knowing you don't have to make a mortgage payment. It's yours free and clear. You will have to continue to save. The reason is you will need to pay property taxes and insurance. These are musts that have to be considered. You will also continue to save to pay for your furniture and all the items you will need for the home. I truly followed this part of the plan. I saved money to buy the kitchen table set I wanted. You should use cash money to buy towels and dishes. Do not get a credit card to purchase these items. These items are not expensive. I actually used the same as cash plans that some of the furniture stores offer to furnish my living room. I worked. I saved the money needed to pay it off in advance so I wouldn't incur interest. If you decide to buy furniture using the same as cash plan, read the contract before signing to make sure you won't have to pay any additional fees if you pay in advance. You may also have family and friends who will help you furnish your place.

As I have realized the benefits of following this plan, I will continue to follow it. I have made some mistakes. That's why I can tell you it's a great plan if you follow it.

At this point, life should be pretty good for you. If you want to hang out with your friends, at this point, you can. You have money available to as much as you like. You will continue to save. Why not? You may decide you want to buy another car. You still do not want to get into debt so you will save and have the money available if you want to get a new car or a new house. You own the items you have now. You can sell them or you can use the house as a rental property and increase your income base that way. Either way, you can continue to save your money. Don't spend it all shopping, partying, and going on trips. **<u>CONTINUE TO SAVE.</u>** You're on your way to becoming a millionaire if you do.

Live With Parents

If you are one of those people who want to stay at home with your parents, there is totally nothing wrong with it if you are helping them and not mulching. In fact, this can be a way for you to help them follow the plan. Whether it's your mom, dad, and you, or you and one parent, it can be done for them too. If you have siblings living with you all, the more, the merrier, and the quicker you can finish the plan. I know there is someone reading this who is thinking why should you invest your money into helping your parents pay off their home. Why not? It's yours also. Chances are they have almost paid it off if you are of working age. Why not give instead of always taking. Imagine the relief you all will experience having paid a home off. Imagine how you all will be able to move on to the goal of saving your money until you become a millionaire or whatever the next goal is. Imagine if you have your parents helping you save to pay for your first home in full when you buy it. They're going to help you in one-way or another anyway. It's a given. You have every reason to do this.

It would be great if as each sibling reaches adulthood that you all work together to help encourage the other to become more financially savvy. I was going to say help each other get a paid for home, but someone isn't going to act right. They're going to want to get everything without having to work for it. They're going to think they're entitled to the benefits without the labor. Never mind.

In the Military

If you are in the military, this is an excellent way to follow the plan. They pay for your housing, uniforms, and your meals. How great is this? You get to sometimes travel to places you may have never thought to go. They cover your basic necessities. In fact, they cover all your necessities because they will give you medical and dental care. It is imperative to them that you are healthy and able to take care of yourself and others in your job.

When you enter the military you will bring your everyday clothing. Those are the things you will wear when you are off duty. You probably shouldn't try to buy a car right away. You may be required to change duty stations. Even if they will pay for vehicle transportation from duty station to station, you may go to a place you will not need a car. Basically, this is a great opportunity to save your money. Wherever you are stationed, you should set aside some money to visit and get to know your surrounding areas. Some of these places you only get to see once in a lifetime. History is being made everyday. It will be amazing to see the changes these places will make over time. Besides, the military has established travel itineraries that are a lot less expensive than if you were planning the trip yourself. I would also encourage you to learn the colloquial language of different countries you visit. It could be of use to you later.

You never know. You may become an interpreter. The world is changing so fast, you almost have to speak a second language at jobs with international connections.

So you're saving your money for a couple of years. Life in the military changes rapidly. You are ordered to different duty stations usually every two to three years depending on your job and the state of the world. When you're just starting out, it may not be a good idea to buy a house. You may or may not choose to live in your hometown, which would be the most likely choice of purchasing a home. If you have been to a place you like, there's no guarantee of when you will get a chance to go back there to spend quality time. It would be a waste of your time in effort.

My advice is to save your money until you are certain of where you are going to live. It won't hurt you to have money in the bank. When you establish that you need a car, pay for it in full. When you've determined it is a wise time to purchase a home, you can pay for it in full too. If you've saved like you should, you will have that luxury and freedom.

You're Married

If you're married, you can definitely follow the plan. If you two work together, you know you can get there faster if you have the same goals. I would like to think there is no reason two people working together to achieve this goal would not be able to make more than twenty thousand dollars a year. The advice is the same as the twenty thousand dollar a year salary if you make fifty or a hundred thousand dollars or more a year. I want to remind you I use twenty as a base amount.

If you're living in an apartment, it's going to be hard to achieve your goal as soon. I know you will not want to live with your parents as newly weds. You can apply for a mortgage. You're going to do the reverse of what I suggest in other areas of this book.

You can get a thirty- year mortgage. You will be aggressive in paying this mortgage by both of you paying a full mortgage payment. You will incur different expenses in purchasing this home. There are a lot of hidden costs in maintaining a home that your parents pay of which you are not aware. I tell you this so you won't think the extra money you may have left from your check can be spent willy nilly. Trust me, this is where a lot of the divorces over money begin.

You will save any money outside of your bills until you have at least enough to replace a water heater. Why a water heater? It is one of the basic needs you will have and probably the most expensive repair you will have as an emergency outside of roof leaks. Getting your kitchen or bathroom remodeled is not an emergency. Do not consider it as such. Do not concern yourself with an endeavor like this even if your real estate agent considers it a great way to make more money in a resale. If you're just moving into a home, your first thought shouldn't be to resale. Your concern should be to make sure you can stay in it. After you have paid it off and you want to do upgrades. Do it. It's such a waste to do upgrades then, you have to foreclose because you cannot afford the upgrades.

If you have a child/ren it will take longer to accomplish your goals because children have needs that will not wait for tomorrow. This does not mean it is impossible. It means it will take a little longer. You will have to be diligent. I recommend doing the plan in three to five years because once you get it started and get it over with, the better off you'll be. The longer you take; I believe you'll stop. You won't think it will work, but it will work if you are aggressive.

CHAPTER TEN

I AM DROWNING IN DEBT

Join the club. Everybody has felt like they were drowning in debt. I can remember feeling that way in college when I had an eight-dollar telephone bill. Crazy I know. So what are you to do? It depends on your situation.

I want to start this section with people who are perhaps married or divorced, older, and have established enough debt where they actually are drowning in debt. So, if you are one of these people, what I want you to do first is get all of your bills together. I want you to get your check stubs for the last two months at least if you have them. If you do not have them, get what you have. We are going to do some calculations. Another thing you will need is as many of your tax returns you may have. You're supposed to keep them for seven years. If you don't have that many it's okay, but there's a lot going on with your money that these documents will reveal to you.

Now, what I want you to do is calculate all of your bills. Write the bill and its amount down on paper so you will remember at what you're looking. You need to calculate expenditures for which you will not have a bill. These will be things such as gas, groceries, impulse shopping and the like.

Next, you're going to calculate how much money you make each month. I suggested two months of pay stubs because some peoples' hours can be more or less depending on the kind of work you do. There are jobs where they send people home early if they're not needed. There are those jobs where you work overtime sometimes. In this case you will get an average of what you make.

Now, I want you to calculate line 37 on your tax returns for all the years you have them available. How close have you almost been to becoming a millionaire already, but you've wasted the money on who knows what or where. I did this one-day, and I could not believe what I saw. How close I have been to becoming a millionaire. Do I have what I would think I would to show for it? No. I would think I would have a bigger house if I were a millionaire. I would have a fancier automobile. I would be traveling right now. Okay, sure, all of this is relative. I have a nice home that I really enjoy living in. I have the same car I bought some time after graduating. I have traveled and taken some very fun trips. So it's not like the money I spent hasn't done some good things. I do pay my tithe and I contribute to charities. It's not like I have lived a horrible life. It's just amazing that if I had known what I know now, how I could have reconfigured my money to do more. I know now so, I'm doing better now.

This is what you're going to do since you believe you are drowning in debt, but still going impulse shopping and charging little nothing of purchases on your credit cards. Isn't it amazing how you believe you're drowning in debt, but instead of reducing your expenditures, you're increasing them? It shouldn't take a genius to figure out that this isn't a good plan. Yet, we do it everyday.

You're going to reconstruct how you pay your bills. You probably have been aimlessly paying them, hoping you'll have enough money when the bill is due. Why do we do that? You know you have bills to pay each month. You go to work every day. You should have calculated which paycheck you will pay each bill based on when the bill is due. This is why some of your leasers allow you to decide at which time of the month you want to pay your bills. This allows you to plan your finances so you won't have problems paying them. Proper planning will allow you to pay your bills like clockwork. This means without any problems under normal situations.

In Maslow's Hierarchy of Survival, clothing and food is top notch. I consider your mortgage to be your first priority. The reason being is you're not going to miss a meal. Most of us could miss a meal or two and it would improve us.

Everyone wants and needs a safe place to live. Also, food can be very inexpensive if you are hungry. You can take twenty-five dollars per person and eat for quite a while if you had to do it. Let's calculate. A five- pound bag of rice to eat for dinner is three dollars. A five-pound bag of grits is two dollars. A tub of margarine or four-sticks of butter is two dollars. A loaf of bread is a dollar and fifty cents. Let's say a jar of peanut butter and jelly is three dollars. A gallon of milk is three dollars. A dozen of eggs are two dollars. You can buy a box or bag of cereal to have for breakfast or as dessert three dollars. Get some fresh fruit for roughage, five dollars. These are the staples needed to feed royalty. If you want to get out of debt, you can and you don't have to starve or become malnourished to do it. You have to have the desire to achieve it first. Then, you must have discipline. It's as elementary as that.

Again, you'll pay your mortgage first. If your bills are late or your money runs short, you always pay your mortgage. All of your bills are paid after your mortgage. I cannot think of a bill that is more important than this one. When you write your check to pay your mortgage, you should do it with happiness because it's the American Dream and you have achieved a pinnacle. If it is more of a burden than a blessing, then you need to sell or downsize to a more manageable payment.

You will get a calendar and mark your due dates for bills on it. You will mark when you get paid. You will at this point determine which check you will use to pay your mortgage first, then all other bills in accordance with their priority. If, your cable or phone has to get cut off, so be it. You don't want to be homeless.

You will determine out of which check you will pay your power and water bills based on when they are due. You will chart this on the calendar. You are calculating this where it will not cause these bills to be late if you don't send them off in time. I know most people are paying bills on-line now, but some people don't. Plus, if your financial resources are low, you may not have the option of having online services in your home.

If you have cable, it is a bill that is not necessary, especially if you are trying to get rid of debt. You wouldn't believe how many people are willing to loose their home, when if they had stopped paying for cable, they could have used this money for paying a bill. Cable, satellite or whatever you use for your television viewing pleasure is not a necessity. When you have determined you are in financial trouble, this is one of the first things to go. They may charge you cancellation fees. If you cannot pay the monthly bill, there's no need to worry about having to pay cancellation fees right now. I don't know why people feel they aren't living if they don't have cable. I have never paid for cable directly until a few years ago. Whether it was charged, as a part of housing is something I haven't had control over. If I had to pay for it, I never had it, even if I didn't have money problems at the time. I would watch the free three and public TV. I would read, write and listen to music. Of course, when I have cable, I watch it. Why not? Besides, I have other things I would prefer to do with my money. Is that sad or what?

If you are drowning in debt, you should cancel your online service. You can send your bills by mail or go on site to the company to pay a bill. If you have enough time to waste playing online, you have enough time to get another job as a life buoy to save you from drowning. It's as simple as that.

Once you're safe and able to play and float in the financial waters, then you can get these things reconnected. These are the things you don't have to have. They are not worth loosing your home over.

You're not drowning in debt because you can't afford your house. You're drowning in debt because you've fooled yourself into believing you have an endless supply of money. When we who are in debt hear it said that credit cards are used for emergency situations and you're supposed to pay any balances off each month, we're thinking whoever said this must be crazy. The majority of us are thinking "our" credit cards are an extension of our salary. When our salary starts to get too tight and we're thinking we can't handle our debt, instead of paying a bill off or getting another job, or dare we stop shopping, we apply for another credit card or two.

You're drowning in debt because you're foolishly acquiring a lot of debt at once without ever paying any of it off. You're not gaining ownership of anything. You probably don't even own the underwear you have on because you've charged it on a credit card. Do you realize how long it will take you to get rid of a small purchase like underwear on your credit card? Sometimes it's until death do you part. Some of you have had your credit cards so long you will celebrate anniversaries of the two of you being together. Some of you have a longer commitment going with your credit card debt than you've been able to maintain with any human relationship.

You're drowning because you're wasting money on things

you really don't have enough time to get any real use. You may have five hundred channels with cable, but you're watching maybe twenty of them and three of them you would get for free anyway. You're spending over a hundred dollars a month for online services and you can get that free at the library if you want to use it. Our government allows you to use their/our computers, books, videos and all sorts of good stuff and they store it for you in their big closet of a library. Once upon a time, I was buying a lot of VHS tapes, CDs, DVDs and books. One day I realized I could continue to buy them, but I would eventually have trouble storing them. It was a waste of money for me to rent them and have to pay late fees. So I started checking them out at the library. Besides, I wasn't getting to read or view the things I was buying. You'll be amazed. Your libraries can order books and viewing materials that you want. You can become a gourmet chef with all the materials they have available or become a financial wiz. Your quality of life can be improved if you were to try to make use of its vast resources.

Cell phones are so convenient. You almost cannot live without one nowadays. Get rid of the phone if you're about to loose your house. It's not a necessity. You can use your landline phone, although, I know you don't want to because all the bill collectors are calling on it. If you are drowning in debt, you don't need it, nor does your spouse or children.

Who are you all calling? If you're at work or school, you should be too busy to talk on the phone. If it's important, there are phones available at these places for you to use. When you get home you shouldn't be using your phones to call each other and you can use the house's landline phone, even if you have fighting teenagers. I don't understand why people don't understand this.

I also don't understand why people text all the time and complain about the bill. I decided some time ago there were certain bills I would not complain about. For instance, I will not complain about paying my mortgage because I wanted a house. I was blessed with it, therefore, I would not complain about it. If I found myself complaining about it, I believe I should sell it. Who complains about being blessed? Stupid people and note that I do not believe in calling people stupid, but you would have to be to complain about a blessing.

We've gotten rid of some unnecessary bills for a person who is drowning in debt. It may be hard to do this, but it is necessary if you want to float. Your children may get mad at you because you are causing them embarrassment by not having the latest phones and gadgets. Ask them if they would be more embarrassed if you all had to live out of your car or in a homeless shelter. There are choices.

Let them know that people usually surround people on the same financial level, so if you're struggling, chances are their friend's parents are also to some degree, but they're not aware that they are or are not admitting to it. Tell your children they can start a new trend by not being burdened with technology or better yet, let them volunteer serving at a shelter so they can see what their options will be if changes aren't made. Let them know you hate it too. It has to be done.

This first month after you have paid your mortgage and discontinued use of the other things you don't need, you should have a few hundred dollars free that you didn't have before. You have plotted on a calendar of how, when, and out of which checks you will be paying all of your necessary bills. By doing this, you should have alleviated some late fees you were incurring before, the source of some of your debt. You should have several hundred dollars available already.

I haven't said it, but you should stop at this very moment using any of your credit cards. You should stop wasting your gas and time impulse shopping. You don't have the internet so you should not be cruising there either trying to find ways to spend money on things you will hardly ever use, but feel you have to have. This should give you some more money and free time for another job to give you more money to pay off your debt or family time.

Some of you may not need to get a second job because your second job may cause you to spend more money. I know you think I don't know. Some of you will get a second job working at a retail store or craft shop because it's something that interests you. You end up spending that check and more besides getting stuff.

If you can make it without a second job, do so. Use this free time you'll have using the stuff you've already bought. Cook in those dishes you bought. Read some of those books you've bought. Build some of that stuff you bought the tools to build or fix. Enjoy your home. Take some time to enjoy these things you've worked hard to purchase.

One of my girlfriends called me one day and asked me what I was doing. I told her I was sitting in my kitchen enjoying looking at the things I had bought to decorate it. She told me I was silly. I hardly ever sat in my kitchen. Some days it was not even seen by me if I bought take-out. I'm learning to make time to enjoy what I've purchased that was waiting for a day when I wouldn't be too busy so I can use them.

Either way, you should be feeling some relief. I'll bet you didn't realize how much money you were wasting on late fees and over the limit fees on your credit cards alone.

The money you are saving by these first changes will be placed in your savings account for a true emergency. I know a lot of financial gurus say to save at least six to eight months for an emergency fund. We will get to that point, but we are not going to do it quite the way they suggest.

I hope you read the Suggestions To Succeed and the Getting

Started chapter because they will have some tips you can use. One in particular is you and your family are going to stop eating out all the time. You're going to start cooking together. You're going to take your lunches to work and school. Note: If you have a teenager who protests this and says they refuse to eat lunch they brought to school. I would give in to this one for health sake. Teenage girls have extreme cases of malnutrition already from eating disorders. This is a battle I would prefer to loose. I know there are people who will say you need to deal with her self-esteem issues. I agree with that too. While you are dealing with that, allocate money for her to do lunch with her friends in the customary way. It's not worth loosing your child. It's not worth her loosing her "dignity" she feels she has. This is such a vulnerable time in their development. Some things they get over, we all have had to, but you don't know what will drive a person at this age to hurt themselves or commit suicide; and we don't want to know. If you have to have business lunches, they should be at the companies expense and/or a tax write- off for you.

If you are drowning in debt and your spouse is not working, this needs to change. If s/he objects and threatens to commit suicide, tell him/her to grow up. When things get better, you can go back to some of the status quo. I do not disagree with a parent staying at home to raise the children. For the time being, they can get a job in the evening or part time at least during the weekends. I know if you're trying to maintain an image for your friends and neighbors and above all an image for yourself, you don't want to do this. If you have to get a job in another neighborhood, do it. It won't last forever. It'll last until you're able to do better and are willing to make better decisions.

The second month, you're going to use the extra money you made from the changes you've made to pay off or reduce the bill you have on your list that's less than one thousand dollars. There are various plans on how to pay your bills off. I suggest balances lower than one thousand dollars because with all these adjustments you've made, you need to see some results fast to make you feel better about the changes you and your family are making.

I understand that some financial plans suggest you pay off the balance with the highest interest rate. It isn't a bad plan if you choose to do it that way, but if the balance is larger than some of the others, you may get disillusioned before you get started.

After you have paid off debts that are less than one thousand dollars, we are going to take a detour that's different than some advice you may have gotten in the past. I want you to start adding all of your extra money from the adjustments you have made to pay off your mortgage.

Normally, you're advised to pay off all credit card debt before you pay your home off.

I'm advising you to pay off your mortgage because of how debt is categorized. If you have read about debt, you know there is secured debt and unsecured debt.

Secured debt is debt that needs collateral to secure the debt if you become delinquent with your payments. In other words, if you don't pay, the bank has something they can take from you to make sure they get their money. Examples are your house and your car.

Unsecured debt is debt that does not require collateral. Credit card debt usually falls in this category. If you do not pay credit card debt, the bank cannot take your house or car. They may put a lien against your home where if you don't clear it up and you sell your house, you or the person who buys your home and doesn't wisely check to see if you have a lien against your house, will have to pay it.

Why is it important for you to know this when paying your

bills? For years I have read this information and did not quite understand it. The reason is it is more important for you to have a house to live in and a car to get you back and forth to work. If your credit card debt isn't paid versus your survival debt, your FICO score will be affected, but you will still have a place to live. With this said, I advise you to place all of your extra money into paying your home off.

You may be thinking this is not only unbelievable, but impossible to do also. It's not if you analyze your annual pay against your mortgage. Generally your mortgage will be three times your salary. If you were to cut back on the expenses I discussed earlier and place all of that extra money towards your mortgage, you can have your home paid in as little as five to six years approximately.

I can tell you're in disbelief still. How? Why would I use my entire check outside of paying my utilities, food, etcetera toward paying my house off? My question would be why haven't we been doing it like this anyway. First of all, it's your home, why wouldn't you want to pay it off. It's not like an apartment. All the value will come to you. It's the best investment you'll ever make. Whether the market goes up or down, you have a place for you and your family to live and it's paid in full.

Second: The best part of this investment is you will not have to pay all the interest you would have paid over the thirty-year term of the loan. In my mortgage agreement it was explained to me that I would have paid almost three times the value of the home in interest payments. That's not how it was stated, but when you read between the lines, that's what my summation of it revealed.

Third: I know you're thinking hey, I get to itemize the interest when I file my taxes each year and I really enjoy the return. Are you serious? You would prefer to file the interest on your return for the next thirty-years instead of avoiding paying that interest?

To my understanding the way a mortgage loan works is you pay the bank and of course there is money going toward the principle. The bank gets its money in the first twenty years and after that even though on your statement it will appear you're paying interest, you're only paying toward the principal. The façade is for the purpose of allowing you to itemize your taxes. They help you keep being ignorant and it makes the world go 'round.

NOTE: When you make additional payments most banks do not consider these payments as future payments toward your loan. They are additional payments you decide to make. You cannot decide to skip one month and say, I paid more last month. It does not work that way.

What if in the course of your life of paying your monthly payments over time, you were to get very sick where you are incapacitated and cannot work or loose your job or both? What will you do when the checks stop coming in and you can't afford your mortgage in addition to your other maintenance. If you loose your home, you will not be able to itemize it on your taxes. It's a safer investment to pay it in full. Go on. Bite the bullet and make these extra payments.

If you are one of the people who continues to not understand why you want to pay off secured debt first, here are some other options for you. This is where I would want you to start after you have paid in full any bills you have less than one thousand dollars and your mortgage, and your cars.

Once you have paid your basic survival bills, you will put all extra money on your credit card bills or any debt you have financed through furniture companies and the like.

You will pay these bills in either of two ways. You can pay the bills starting with the smaller balances regardless of the interest rate. Some people may prefer this because it helps wipe the slate clean faster. It makes you feel like you're accomplishing something.

The other choice would be to pay the bill with the highest interest rate because you will save more money that way, or rather, you will reduce the amount of money you pay in interest.

After you have paid off at least six months of bills using either system, take your family out to a moderately priced restaurant to relax. You will not be spending all the money you would be using for bills for the meal. Note: I did say moderately priced restaurant. Then, you will continue, as you were previously with whichever system you chose.

You will keep your credit in good standing and get rid of your enormous debt load with either system.

One thing I didn't mention that you should cut out if you are doing it is the extra curricular activities the children are participating in. You can let them continue at least one they are good in or that they simply like. These activities can be expensive and draining. Some that they don't have any talent in should be eliminated. Believe it or not, they may be relieved. Too many guys are on sports teams because their dads have these high hopes of them becoming professionals. Dads, be realistic, if you're not a pro, chances are it's not in the genes. Dad, if you are in the pro, it still may not be in the genes. You weren't the only one who contributed DNA.

It may take some time before you can get everything paid off, but if your debt is about the same as your yearly salary, you can get it paid off in as little as four years if you cut back and get more income coming into the house. Basic knowledge, spend less bring in more income. Don't forget to tithe and pay offerings.

You live and you learn. I am. Hopefully with the sacrifices you've made, you won't have to relearn this lesson. I have had to repeat a few mistakes several times before I learned the lesson. I'm hoping you can learn from my mistakes. If you make the mistake again, you won't be the first person to ever do that either. Join the club. There are plenty of members just like you. Life is for living and learning.

I know I've probably made this seem too simple. It is. If you borrow these people's money, you have to pay them back. It's as simple as that. You have to change. You have to start paying cash for stuff, or at least not go into debt. You do not impress yourself or anyone else by using your credit card to buy another pair of shoes or earrings you'll hardly ever wear because you're wearing the same outfits anyway. Stop the madness.

I know we get caught up in watching TV where we see these people wearing new clothes every episode. They are borrowing these clothes from designers and stores for these shows. Some have budgets and clothing allowances. It's fine if you can afford it. If you cannot afford it, don't burden yourself with it.

In my case, and you may be like me, I just like the stuff. I like the trinkets and novelty items. I like little girlie stuff. I like bows and ruffles and bright pretty colors. If you're guy, you may like having the tools and gadgets and man toys. It's okay. Some of us don't do it to impress. We like it. What I'm learning is pay in cash. I have to chant it in my mind sometimes. Pay in cash. Pay in cash. Pay in cash.

CHAPTER ELEVEN

SHOULD I SELL MY HOUSE

I totally disagree with the financial gurus who tell people to sell their homes and go live in an apartment because they have credit card debt. Credit card debt is unsecured debt. You're not going to loose your home if you do not pay it.

I do believe the banks will continue to give credit cards to people who do not qualify for them. You should not be lying about your income to increase your chances of getting more credit card debt. Some of you know you are fudging the numbers to increase your chances.

Technically, if your debt is less than your yearly income, you can afford to pay your bills off without filing for bankruptcy. This excludes your mortgage. Even if your debt exceeds your yearly salary by two years, you can make it. If it exceeds two years salary minus your mortgage, then it's getting kind of dicey.

All the same, the only time I would say you should sell your home is if you got your home with an ARM loan, it has adjusted and you cannot make the payments. The reason I would suggest it with this type of loan is because if you cannot get your mortgage refinanced, your mortgage can become outrageous and unaffordable. My first piece of advice would be to never get an ARM loan. They are dangerous because no one knows the future. This kind of loan is speculative on what the future holds. With a traditional loan, your house payment itself will not change, but your insurance payments and property taxes will cause the payment to adjust.

You do not need to sell your home even if that means stopping the payment on your credit cards. This includes if you have an ARM. You will pay your mortgage, utilities and buy food. It may take a while to sell. You may have to get an additional job to help you through this time. You have to know when you go through a rough time it will not last forever. Keep moving. Keep working. Keep trying. It happens to the best of us and you are one of the best.

CHAPTER TWELVE

I NEED TO AVOID FORECLOSURE

Yes you do. If your home is about to go into foreclosure, you need to stop everything right now. You need to stop all outgoing expenses. Every penny you have will have to go toward the mortgage.

You will stop shopping. You will stop memberships to any clubs and organizations. You will stop participating in any hobbies. You will stop going out to eat. You will cancel your cable. You will cancel your phone services. Your children will not go to private school.

You will return items you have bought recently that have the tags and which you have the receipts to the stores. You will not buy one video game, a beer, or a cigarette. Every penny you have will have to go toward a mortgage payment.

I know some of you are in such dire straits you don't believe you have the time to read the rest of this book. You're going to skip right to this chapter. You would think I wouldn't have to tell someone who is about to go into foreclosure any of the above things, but I know I do. I know there are people out there who are living in cars because they would not stop their cable services or phone service in order to maintain an image. I know there are people who have memberships to gyms and organizations they don't participate in where the charges are being taken out on their credit cards each month and they have forgotten about it. There are some of you who are shopping like nothing's happening to you. Stop it!

First of all, if you're working everyday, but it seems like money for your bills is coming up short each month, the last bill to be short is your mortgage. Your mortgage should be the first bill you set aside money. If your money were to come short for your mortgage payment one month, save what you have from the first month and add it to the second month. You may be behind, but it will help you avoid going into foreclosure. Use all of the money you would be spending on whatever else to get your payments caught up.

I know someone out there is thinking, even your tithe and offering? Your tithe and offering is not a bill. The tithe and offering is supposed to be taken out of your check first. This is not going to be your excuse not to pay your tithe and offering.

If you were paying your tithe and offering first and handling your business like you should, this wouldn't be happening to you in the first place. What tithing and offering does is establish a disciplined system of handling your money. It makes you look at the money you make to pay it first; and then, you will consider how and when paying everything else. It lets you stay aware of what you can and cannot afford. There are lots of people who spend their paychecks aimlessly. You are probably one of those people. I have been one of those people.

There are lots of people who do not pay tithes and offering because they believe they are taking care of the preacher. His salary does come from the tithes, but they are used for more than that. They are used to pay for the church and it's utilities. They are used to benefit families.

You have to make a decision as to whether or not you pay your tithe. If you pay it, the Lord may give you divine debt cancellation or an outside source for paying that bill. If you pay your bill instead of your tithe, you won't become one of these families the tithes and offerings have to benefit.

Don't look at your tithes and offerings as a bill you have to pay God. You cannot beat God giving, no matter how you try. The more you give, the more he gives to you. This is according to the words in the Bible and the song written by Doris Akers entitled, You Can't Beat God Giving.

CHAPTER THIRTEEN

HELOC

Home Equity Lines Of Credit. That's what HELOC means if you didn't know. These are not increases in your income. These are not ways to hide bad debt to be written off into your mortgage and itemized on your income taxes. I know this is what you're doing with them. If you don't want to get the Signature Loan or another credit card, a lot of homeowners use their home as a line of credit. There are so many tricks and loopholes we use to acquire stuff. Do you really need this stuff? So many people will get second and third mortgages to pay for stuff they could use cash for and come out better off. You think you're taking the easy way out when you're really making it harder for yourself.

Do you really need to update your kitchen? Do you know if times get hard for you financially and you cannot pay this loan back the bank can take your home. Is it worth it?

Do you need that new truck? One time I did advise someone to use his home as a line of credit. I did not know what he was talking about. It sounded like a good deal. He would buy the truck. The money used would look like it's a part of the house payment and could be itemized on his taxes. It would be better than financing through the dealership or the bank because of the interest rate and because it can be itemized. I would advise with my knowledge now to save for the truck and buy it outright. He didn't need it anyway.

CHAPTER FOURTEEN

LEASING A CAR

A person who leases a car is a slave to image. The only way I could see where leasing a car makes sense is you already have a working vehicle that is paid off, you own your house without any kind of mortgage or home equity lines of credit, and you have lots of discretionary income to throw away.

There are so many rules to follow to avoid any extra fees. You lease a car to have the latest of the greatest. If you must maintain a certain image and this is the way, happy leasing.

CHAPTER FIFTEEN

CREDIT CARDS

We have been convinced we have to have them. We don't. If someone told you to give them a hundred dollars and they would give you ten dollars back, would you do it? You say no without hesitation, but every time you apply for and use credit cards, you are agreeing to this. Don't worry. I'm not exempt. I fell for the okidoke too.

I remember years ago one of my girlfriends told me she did not have any credit card bills. I wanted to be debt free back then and was striving to be, but I did not understand how she was operating her life without one credit card. I hope she continued to live that way.

She didn't agree with the practice of using credit cards for everyday ordinary purchases where she should and could use cash. I'll say I've gained information for this plan in normal life experiences. She was right. We use our credit cards to buy candy.

Do you not have the cash to buy candy? If you're saying you do not like carrying cash on you. I understand. I feel the same way. You can use your debit card. It's wise to have some money on you just in case. I had to learn that too. You never know what circumstances will require it.

I believe I can berate you all day and night about credit card usage and it's not going to change you if you believe you need to get those points and sky miles. I've been there.

Now I'm getting my miles converted to magazine subscriptions. That's what happens to unused points and sky miles.

Do you know how you're manipulated into getting into credit card debt? I know for me, having a credit card seemed like the cool thing to have. It allows you to buy stuff even if you don't have the money. How cool is that?

I got my first credit card while I was in college. I lied to get it. They lied by letting me have it. Only junior and seniors students were supposed to get them at that time. I was a freshman. While you're in college, they don't care what year you are. If you cannot pay your bill, they expect your parents will cover you. Their motive is to gain you as a lifelong customer.

The trick, regardless of how you got your credit cards, is your initial purchase is probably small. Your first minimum payment is probably no more than twenty dollars. Wow! Who can't afford to pay that? When you have payments as small as this, you can get about four more cards and you may have a hundred dollar bill to pay a month. That's not a major dent in your finances, right? Then, you get involved in other big ticket purchases like a car because you'll need a car to get you to your job so you can pay your credit card bills.

It all seems so easy until you realize you need insurance on the car. You have to get maintenance done on the car, plus window tint, rims and a booming system. That's a high tech radio for those of you who do not know what a booming system is.

You don't want to hear what your parents are telling you about anything, so you move into an apartment. Now you have to pay for your food, laundry maybe, cable, phone, to get your hair done, and your nails "did". By now, you're sucked into the trappings of the debt cycle. You wanted to be grown and this is what grown, or being an adult in America looks like. As an adult you get to do what you want when you want. There's a price for it. You have to pay to play.

CHAPTER SIXTEEN

SAME AS CASH

I have used this method to purchase items. It is a very good way to go if you do what you're supposed to do. To get the same as cash value you have to pay the balance before the end of the terms and conditions you applied. For instance, I purchased furniture on the six- month plan. I divided my balance by five months instead of six. I did not want to wait until the last minute in case something unfortunate occurred to prevent me from paying according to the terms I had applied. By the time I was sent a bill, which included the interest I would have to pay if I didn't pay according to the agreement, I ran to pay them that last payment ahead of time. If you're a day late, you will have to pay the balance with the interest included. That's the way it works.

CHAPTER SEVENTEEN

READ THE FINE PRINT

When you're purchasing with cash, the fine print is IN GOD WE TRUST. When you're using credit cards or requesting loans, there are loads of fine print and terms you have to almost have a law degree to read and understand. Read the fine print. We're always told this and the majority of us rarely do. You need to know what you're agreeing to do. There are loans that will penalize you if you pay it off early. There are loans that will require you to pay all of the interest whether you pay off early or use the full term. You need to know if advanced payments will be considered as future payments or as additional principle added toward the payment for that month. Additional payments on your mortgage like I suggest you pay toward paying your house off faster **ARE NOT** considered as future payments. If you miss paying one month, these payments will not count. You cannot say, well I paid extra so I don't have to pay this amount.

CHAPTER EIGHTEEN

CO-SIGNING

I'm trying to think what can I say to you to get you not to co-sign on a loan with your friends. I know you're going to co-sign with your folks so I'm not going to bother with that except to tell you this; whatever you co-sign for, make sure it's something you want if you end up having to make the payments on it.

When you co-sign for someone you may learn an invaluable lesson. The cliché, no good deed goes unpunished. Sometimes you can try to do a good thing for a person and it will end up hurting you. The interesting thing about it is they will act like they did you a favor.

If the bank is saying they need a co-signer and they're older than nineteen, chances are something's going on that makes them think they're not going to get their money. If they don't think they're going to get their money, I hope you have a better system than theirs to insure you get your money back.

CHAPTER NINETEEN

THE THING WITH BANKS

The purpose of a bank according to the average person is for you to get money when you need it. It is a place to store money you don't want to spend. I don't know how they marketed that idea and convinced people to stop saving it under the mattress.

The main project of the bank is to make more money off of your money. I've heard suggestions of getting to know your banker so if you need something they will be familiar with you. They are not trying to be your friend. Besides, the employees' change so often, it's a mute point to do that at most banks.

You have to approach the bank for what they are, moneymakers. They are not going to loan any money to you unless they are getting something out of it. It's as simple as that.

They will charge you fees for any and every little thing. Don't take it personally when you get charged fees to get to use your money. They charge everyone who has a little money there. The larger the amounts of money you have stored with them or that you get processed there may alleviate some of your fees, but other than that, the fees will get you.

You may wonder, why isn't the bank advising you to pay off your house the way this book is recommending. They will not tell you this because they make the money that helps them operate off of the interest from your loans and credit cards, plus all the other fees they charge you. When you buy a house for one hundred thousand dollars, they make approximately two hundred thousand dollars. Do you understand why it's to their advantage not to tell you this?

CHAPTER TWENTY

SHOPAHOLIC

Hello, my name is Kathryn and I'm a shopaholic. Oh yea. This is I. I have been this person. I do not shop because I have emotional drama. I shop because I enjoy it. I simply enjoy it. I enjoy finding unique trinkets and novelty items. I enjoy feeling fabrics and different textures in my hand. I like exploring the creations so many designers of different genres of crafts have created. I enjoy it when there are a few people or crowds galore. I enjoy shopping. I try not to do a lot of online shopping because it's too easy to spend all of your money without ever leaving your home. I have to have some limits. I also balance my shopping because the priority is to pay my bills first so I can have a place to hold all of my collections.

Being that I have confessed that I am a shopolic, it means I am supposed to change my ways. There are times when I have changed. There are times when I will save and not shop. That's usually because I can't find anything I like, but hea, I was saving. Seriously, there have been times when I was totally debt-free. Then, I would become weak and succumb to my old evil habit in spite of what needs should be the priority. I would justify my spending by saying I work hard. I will manipulate and rearrange my money to get what I want because there will always be another check.

There are cases where there are no other checks though. Economic situations may cause job lose. This is what I tell myself to motivate me to do right in the good times, but it doesn't always work. I've gone so far as to tell myself I need to be prepared in case a tragedy like Hurricane Katrina, Greensburg, Kansas or a devastation like that were to occur in my life. I need to be prepared. I need to be prepared not just to help myself, but if others need aid, I need to have money to help them also. I've thought about all kinds of family tragedies that could happen. I, you, we need to take the initiative to have money saved so we will be prepared.

It's hard not to shop. In our society, we have a different occasion to shop for each month. There are so many commercials advertising the latest cars and clothes. The shows we watch are advertisements for how we should live our lives, decorate our homes, and they dictate the foods we eat. No one is exempt.

We set up expectations of how we want to live our lives in the leisure of luxury. It's not that we cannot. We can. You can. I can. What we have to do is prioritize our life in the way we spend money.

We live paycheck to paycheck not because we have to, but because that is as far as we plan our lives. Look at it this way, instead of planning your life until your next paycheck; plan your life over the lifetime of your paychecks. This is what I want you to understand. If your salary is fifty thousand dollars a year, over a twenty- year period you will have earned a million dollars. If this is you, what do you have to show for it? If you are in your twenties and you have a job that pays you fifty thousand, or one hundred thousand dollars a year; and you work forty years, you will have earned two million or four million dollars. This is not including raises and bonuses. The dilemma that comes with earning this amount of money is we have an image we believe this amount of money must proliferate.

I've thought about what it is we have to spend our money on

each month. You have to pay for utilities, food, gas, etcetera, until you die. You pay your mortgage. You buy a car. You buy furniture. Most people don't buy new furniture every year. What is the real value of a sofa if you keep it forever? You'll pretty much get the value out of it. My point here is this, there are certain things you don't have to purchase often in our day- to- day existence. Most people furnish their homes and they will not buy new furniture for years. Where is that money going after you've bought your furniture, paid off your car? Are you saving it?

Most of our money is wasted on paying interest on debt for stuff we've had for years. Or we're spending our money on little trinkets and what-nots. If we were to save our money in our early years of earning and purchase items with cash, we could have money saved to live a leisurely life of luxury instead of giving this lifestyle to the Joneses.

I wish there was some magic thing I could tell you to rid you of shopping using your credit cards except to say don't do it. Wait until you have all the important things taken care of and then, save some money with which to shop. The important thing is to not spend all your money on shopping. Save most of it. As my Dad told me when I was a little girl, "Don't spend every dime you get at the store."

CHAPTER TWENTY-ONE

PAYDAY LOANS AND CAR TITLES

Don't do this. I know it's hard to tell a single parent who has children not to do this. This is not just for single parents because a lot of you are doing this. We are struggling trying to find ways to increase our salaries. This is not a smart way to do it.

Do you realize you are giving so much of your check away my doing this? You need to get a better plan for paying your bills. You know what's due each month. I know you want to have fun. You need to plan your life better so you won't keep giving your hard earned money away.

CHAPTER TWENTY-TWO

BANKRUPTCY AND DEBT CONSOLIDATION

I do not believe I can tell you to or not to file for bankruptcy or debt consolidation. It's a personal decision you have to make after evaluating your situation. This is what I will say. If you're going to choose to pay your creditors, your credit will be ruined for seven years. If this were the case, would it be better to try to pay them off over that time yourself and build your credit back up to good standing? Each situation is different. This is something the individual has to decide.

What probably makes a person file for bankruptcy or debt consolidation is dealing with those irritating phone calls from creditors. You can try to set up a plan with your creditors before filing for bankruptcy or debt consolidation. This may get you a good deal.

What you'll need to do is calculate your monthly income minus your basic living needs to find out how much you have left over to spend on your bills. You'll calculate all your bills and divide them by the amount of money you have left to spend on them. Whatever this total is, you will arrange to pay your creditors. You can also ask them to lower your interest rate. If these ideas do not work for them, maybe it is best to file for bankruptcy or debt consolidation.

In this book, I am trying to show a way to avoid having to make this decision. It's a new way of thinking. We all have to decide what we think is best for us.

CHAPTER TWENTY-THREE

DATING MONEY

A lot of people who are at the typical dating age will not think they should follow this plan. This is the very best time to follow the plan. This is the time you can avoid getting bogged down in the living paycheck- to- paycheck arena.

It is possible to take a person out on a date while you are saving. You can go out to a movie and eats. You don't have to go to the most expensive restaurant in town. You shouldn't be doing that on the first date anyway. In fact, it's becoming very popular to go on lunch dates so you can get away quicker if there's a need. Lunch menus at some restaurants are cheaper then dinner. The movie matinees are reduced prices. You can always rent a movie or get one from the library and have a casual meal at home. You can let your date know you're trying this financial plan with hopes it'll be understood and maybe you'll get a partner who is willing to stay with you and not think you're a cheapskate.

CHAPTER TWENTY-FOUR

WEDDING MONEY

Paying a million dollars for a wedding does not ensure that a couple will stay married any more than if you were to go to the court house to get a license, like everyone has to do anyway. I made an agreement with myself that I would not have a big wedding if I did not have a house or if I did not have money set aside to get a home. I, and anyone who knows me would not believe I would make an agreement like that with myself. Yes, I am a typical girl. I wanted all the fru-fru and regalia that comes with a wedding. I made this decision one day upon hearing that there are people who have budgets for their weddings that could pay for a home. Some of these people have these weddings, but they don't stay married longer than a year. If I were to pay that much money for a wedding, I would have to stay married long enough to get my money's worth, whatever that means and however long that might be. Yes, it may be hell, but I would learn that lesson.

You may not agree with this. I would hope you would at least agree with me to want to have a home to live in after the wedding more so than having a grand event that can be done for a mere one hundred dollars or less.

It's a wonderful thing to have your dream wedding. It's a once in a life- time event. It's supposed to be according to the traditional wedding vows. You may think you'll have plenty of opportunities to get a house. This may be true.

You will have to live happily ever somewhere after the wedding.

In reading this book, my advice would be to save the money for your wedding. Pay for it in cash. People act like paying in cash hurts more than using a credit card when you actually pay more when you use credit cards.

The thing about weddings that baffles me is people always like to get so stressed about them. The most stressful thing about getting married to me should be .... I don't know. So many people have gotten married for so many years, it should all be worked out by now. You shouldn't be stressing over whether you're marrying the right person. That should be known before the proposal. Probably the most stressful thing should be setting the date because you will have to change the date if the venue you've chosen is booked.

I think most girls have been planning their wedding day forever. You know the colors of the flowers and the maids' dresses. You know where you want to be married because the wedding is usually held where the bride chooses without any argument. Okay so the details that are being argued over are done so for tradition sake I guess. Either way, there's no reason to let the budget get outrageous. You can plan the perfect wedding, and pay your life's savings for it, and something is not going to go as perfectly as you had planned. It may be the very thing you invested the most money. How upset would you be if you spent all your money, and everything doesn't go according to plan? You still have your spouse, which is the most important thing. You could have had more of your money too.

CHAPTER TWENTY-FIVE

MARRIED MONEY

It amazes me how money is an inanimate object, but it causes so many of the world's perils. It is said that money is the number one reason most people get divorced. Of course we all look for something or someone to blame for our problems. Being that money is inanimate, I'm sure it doesn't mind.

In an Ebony magazine, I saw a cartoon of a couple getting married. In the caption above the groom's head it read, "I sure am glad to get some help paying the bills. Above the bride's head it said, "I'm sure glad I don't have to work anymore." Need I say more? This miscommunication about money will surely cause lots of problems if not a divorce.

It doesn't have to cause a divorce. The first reason it shouldn't is if the couple took the traditional wedding vows, you vowed to stay married for richer or for poorer. So the question comes of when is it necessary to get divorced over money?

In life, when the couple's beliefs are such polar opposites, someone is going to have to change because his or her expectations will not be met. It would be great if this cartoon wasn't so realistic and people were marrying for love and all it involves instead of the conveniences of their money being pooled together. It would have been wise for this couple to talk about their expectations before marrying. Marriage does involve money because love does not pay the bills. It doesn't have to be as difficult to mix love and money as we make it.

When I was single, I always wondered why it seemed like married people acted like they were struggling to survive financially as much if not more than single people. I asked married people lots of questions and took notes because I didn't want this to affect my marriage, the conclusion I was told comes to this: most couples are continuing to live like they're single instead of married. You would think a married couple could live very well with the commingling of two incomes. If they commingled the two incomes they could. The truth is, they aren't.

You would think couples would do better financially since they don't have to pay two different rents or mortgages, utilities, etc. This can add up to several hundreds or thousands of dollars saved depending on where you live. So what happens to this "extra" money? Instead of pooling the money and getting rid of debt, most couples are creating more debt because they believe this extra money will allow them to get more or bigger toys. They sometimes get bigger homes. They may get a more expensive automobile, or two more. They get to live the "good life" because they have someone else to help carry the load. This results in the drowning in debt and the trip toward divorce.

I have talked to too many people who have married because they wanted someone to help pay the bills, or they needed someone to help them leave their parents home or any other reason than love. So how can these people work together instead of as enemies? They each have their own agenda.

What I can advise a couple is to get together on the common goals you have without question. Before you spend any of your money, the two of you should come together to decide how to pay your bills. You will have to pay a mortgage or rent and utilities whether you live together or are separate.

For whatever reasons couples determine they can't trust their spouses with their money, I don't know or understand. I guess some of it simply is a matter of making money after having to get money from parents, and being able to decide how you want to spend your money instead of having someone tell you what to do. This may explain some things, but it slows down the process of getting goals accomplished if you do not work together with your spouse.

If you two work together you can get out of debt and work toward the goal of becoming a millionaire if not multi-millionaire. The goal is still achievable even if one of you does not come on board. It's more delightful if you work as enlightened married people instead of as roommates.

As a couple, you will follow the plan at whichever stage the two of you are together. If you're just getting started, use that scenario. This is beneficial because, where you could have been starting out alone, you will have some help. Let's change the scenario a bit. Let's say you do not want to begin your married life living with your parents. This makes sense. You are both of age to sign a contract. Go get yourselves a starter home. I would advise you to get it based on only one salary. I do not think you should get it based on both of your salaries if you are going to be financing the home. The reason is if something happens to one of you, you two will still be able to afford your home. You can always upgrade when you have this one paid off.

In a lot of situations, if you can afford to, the husband pays the mortgage and the major household bills, if not all of the bills. The wife may pay a utility bill or two and her car payment. This is where this plan is going to differ.

Say you're doing it the traditional way. The husband is going to continue to pay as is. He will if his income allows, pay additional money toward the mortgage. The wife is going to pay her car note and she will begin to pay the remainder of her income toward the mortgage also.

If you're in an area where you can purchase a starter home for let's say fifty thousand dollars. What if you both make minimum wage? You will make more than twenty thousand dollars a year? Your mortgage would be about four hundred dollars a month. This depends on your credit history. Your salary a month would be about seventeen hundred dollars a month between the two of you. This depends on your deductions. This seems like a lot of money if you've never made any. You have this extra money and you think you can go and buy the world. Don't just yet. What you will do is after paying your basic living expenses of your utilizes, food, gas, etcetera you will save one month's salary. Then, you will use the rest of your money each month to pay toward the mortgage. You can have your home paid off in as little as four years if you are aggressive in paying the mortgage. Can you believe it? If the home is seventy five thousand, you can still have it paid off in as little as six to seven years. You can start furnishing your home by buying your furniture after you have saved the money or do the same as cash plan. Try furnishing one room at a time so you don't go into debt overload.

This will give you two so much freedom. This is a way where even in today's society; you do not have to have two incomes in order to make it. At this point, if the wife or the husband wants, and you two agree, either can become a stay at home spouse or parent if s/he likes.

When you decide you want a bigger home, you can save the difference of the amount you will have to add to the home you want after you sell this home you own. This way you're never buying more than you can afford. The wife can continue to work and the two of you can continue to save your way toward a million dollars. Don't forget to have some fun while you're saving. Always give your tithe and offering.

If you're drowning in debt, you start at the drowning in debt stage. There's hope.

Sometimes there are problems in this situation because one of you is blaming the other for putting you in debt. This may be true that one of you is at fault. No one person is perfect. No one is going to go through this life unscathed. I hope you can find a way to forgive and move on.

If you cannot get your partner to get on board with the plan, you can do it alone. You can make sure all of your household bills are paid, then, you can begin to pay off your small personal bills. After you pay off your bills, you can begin to pay off the mortgage. You're probably thinking there is no way you're going to pay off the mortgage alone. Okay, besides the point that you're living there too is a good reason to make extra payments. Unless you're planning to get divorced, you will be living there. Even if you're planning to get divorced, if you share children with your spouse, they will need a place to live. If you do not have children, you and your spouse will have to divvy the property anyway so it won't be a total lost. I don't know, pay fifty percent of the balance. If you're a man and you're thinking there's no way I'm going to pay a mortgage off and allow her to keep it and put me out. If you're a man and you have children with her, it will happen anyway, unless you can gain full custody. If these are the considerations you're contemplating that are delaying you from becoming debt-free, your debt isn't your biggest problem. I will discuss marital issues beyond money in the book I'm working on entitles, Love is a Gamble, Marriage is Forever.

Married people have so many options with this plan. You can use all of your discretionary income to increase your mortgage payments. You can opt to use one of your checks to pay household expenses and use the other entire check to pay the mortgage. You can both pay an entire mortgage payment out of each of your checks each month. There are so many options.

Some people believe because you're married you should get all of your credit combined and your bank accounts. It really will be the decision you and your spouse have to make. It has to benefit both of you. I thought this too. One day I was told it's sometimes better not to do this. If you've messed up your money, at least you didn't mess up your spouses credit also.

If money is the cause for so many divorces, do you think if you follow one of these choices it can save your marriage. I know there are so many people who will stay with a spouse who commits infidelity. There are cases where spouses have remained together when a spouse has beaten them or gone so far as to try to kill them. Yet, there are people who will divorce because your spouse does not know how or refuses to balance the checkbook. Come on. That's crazy.

I know there are other issues. I know there are men who are insecure when their wives earn more money than they do. There are people who have gambling problems or spouses who are dealing with drug additions, alcoholism, and so forth. Some problems are bigger than money and may not need to be included when talking about it.

If your spouse cannot balance their checkbook or overspends occasionally, it may not be just cause to get rid of them. You are the person who determines what you can and cannot take. If it helps you avoid killing them, it's better to get divorced.

CHAPTER TWENTY-SIX

STAY AT HOME MOMS

If you do not have children, but you know you want to and you want to be a stay at home mom, start planning for it now. I'm serious when I say right now as you're reading this book. You need to begin a plan to have money set aside for taking care of a baby's need. You may not even be married or pregnant. This makes it a better reason to plan ahead. Take the initiative. Be proactive.

The reason I give this advice is, how many women you know who have gotten pregnant, whether they were married or not, who were abandoned by the baby's daddy. Prepare so this won't be a lesson you will have to learn. There is no guarantee you will get child support even if the man is wealthy. Women and children suffer too often in this world when it comes to finances. You don't want you or your child to suffer unduly because you didn't plan ahead.

Start planning and saving now. You know you will need pampers and formula. Besides sleeping, pooping and eating are a given with a baby. You can save by using clothe diapers, but that can be disgusting and time consuming. You can breastfeed. Some people do not have success with it, so it may not go as planned. A lot of the clothing and baby furniture is unnecessary. It's fun to buy all of that stuff, but so unnecessary. I did not buy a lot of the stuff because I finally listened and took the advice of my friends who told me you buy that stuff, but they grow so fast, you don't use most of it.

Besides the items I got at my showers, I made sure I kept plenty of pampers. I did not buy a changing table. I figured we would change our baby wherever we were. There was no guarantee I would go to her bedroom or wherever the changing table would be kept. We did not buy a walker for her. We played with her practicing walking by holding her hands. It wasn't that we were being that cheap. We enjoyed playing with her on the floor and she enjoyed it also. I confess. I did buy her plenty of books. She may not be able to read all of them for some time even though I think she's a genius.

I buy a lot of clothes at the end of the season for the next year. I had someone advise me not to do this because you don't know what size they'll be. My calculations have been pretty good. I trust the designers who made the clothes have researched average baby sizes. They know their stuff. My baby is growing at an average rate, so it's working out. If something doesn't work out, I give it away. It's not like the clothing is an investment. All the same, save if you know you're the kind of person who will go overboard.

Another very important thing I will add here is make sure you get short-term disability. You have to get it before you get pregnant. If you don't it will be considered as a pre-condition and they probably won't cover you. You want this so that you will be able to stay off work during your maternity leave without stressing about money. Check with insurance companies about their requirements. Some stipulations are you have to be a full time employee and your coverage is based on your income. They won't allow you to become a millionaire in those two months.

Another reason you will want to be insured is you don't know if you will get sick while carrying the baby. You do not need any extra stress at this time. As I advised earlier, it would be wise to have all of your bills paid off so you do not have to worry about finances. You can enjoy being pregnant and the birth of your baby. Hopefully, the financial stresses that cause marital problems will be none existent for you. Too many men have left women with newly born babies. Do not let this happen to you. Plan and prepare.

Looking at the positive side of this situation, if you're married and you and your husband know you want to have children. Try using either your check or your husband's check for the household expenses. Then, use the other check to pay the mortgage using the entire check. Depending on how much your mortgage is and your checks, you can have your mortgage paid off in four years or so. After you finish paying your mortgage in full, you can start paying off any other bills you have.

CHAPTER TWENTY-SEVEN

HAVING CHILDREN

If you have children whether you're raising them alone or with a spouse it takes planning and preparation. You know which activities you want your children to participate in. Most of these activities require fees and equipment. Start saving in advance for these fees. You can limit the activities because you don't want to spend your entire life savings on a pastime that the child probably doesn't enjoy anyway.

Daycare is expensive. If you're going to work, you're going to have to pay it. It's possible if you know someone who is a stay at home mom, she may be willing to take care of your children for a little less than a daycare. You will not get the tax write off you would get with a daycare facility. I would weigh the pros and cons and see if you're paying more money to keep the daycare facility open than you're bringing home. Depending on how much money you have left from your check after you pay daycare, you may decide you can work a part time job in the evening or on the weekend. A lot of jobs operate almost on a twenty-four hour shift. There are a lot of them where you can work an early or late shift. It's possible you and your spouse may option to have one of you work day shift and the other will work the night shift.

In this book I am trying to show you where if you make some sacrifices for a few years, you don't always have to have a two-income family. The choice is always yours to make.

You know children require new clothes often because they grow so fast until the teen years for some. Some people get clothes from discount stores, thrift stores, and consignment shops. You can get some really good deals. It is good to get the child a new outfit sometimes even if you have an older child that can pass hand me downs. Everyone needs to experience having new things some times. It could dampen a child's self esteem if they never get anything new for themselves.

If you're not a person who is going to pay for your children to wear the latest fashions, you can always allow them to have a job when they become of age. They can use their money to buy their clothing and pay their expenses. This will allow you more money to take care of the household.

The plan in this book if followed will allow you to have the savings to decide how you want to raise your child without stressing over how they can be happy and you not having to worry about how you're going to pay for it. When you have your mortgage paid off and your car is paid in full, you own your stuff. It frees you from not getting to enjoy your children and the joy they bring.

A lot of people start saving for their children to go to college as soon as they are born. How great is this? This is what I am encouraging you to do for yourself. Start foreseeing what you want and saving for it before you need it. If you'll look at the entire scope of this plan, you'll see that if you were to get rid of your major debt of your house and cars, you will save your money. This money saved, whether you set it aside in designated accounts like a college fund, retirement, or in different family member's names, it's a savings all the same. The money will be there when you need it.

CHAPTER TWENTY-EIGHT

COLLEGE MONEY

If you have graduated from college and you are reading this because you are thinking I am going to give you a plan to get rid of your college loan debt, here it is. Pay those people their money. If you need a plan to pay it off sooner, pay larger payments than they require of you. There's no scheme to avoid paying debt. If you used the goods, you have to pay for them.

If you're a college student who wants a plan to avoid having student loan debt, I have one for you. Instead of using all the money you get from your job to hang out and eat out and lay out with your friends, use some of it to pay off your student loans. You can use some of the money you earn from your summer job also.

Another thing you can do to help reduce college costs is go to a community college to take your core classes. English, Math, Western Civilization, Economics, and Biology are transferable subjects. You can take these classes during the summer. You can start as early as the summer before your senior year. You should save money to pay for these classes. Do not get a loan or apply for a credit card to pay for everything. You may be thinking you don't want to have to spend your cash on these expenses. Whether you pay for them now or later, you'll have to pay for them. If you get the loan or use the credit card, you'll actually pay more for them later.

There are schools now where you can take advanced classes. You will be a sophomore in college when you graduate from high school. If you can get into one of these programs, it will be great.

Please don't do like I did. I did not apply for one scholarship. Being that I was in college, it meant I was somewhat smart. I could have used my smarts and applied for a scholarship. There are so many scholarships available and you have some many sources to search for them. There was a scholarship available if you were left-handed. I'm left-handed and did not want to have to write another left-handed paper using the right side of my brain. The result: having to work extra to pay for my dumb mistake. It happens. I'm over it for me. I want you to make better choices than I made. Perhaps the first better choice is to not be lazy and self-sabotage.

My Mom tried to help me avoid some of the college debt I acquired. She suggested to me I stay home and go to the community college to save some money. I would have saved money on housing, food, and books. The cost of your books in college is astronomical when you're broke.

I should have taken her advice, but I didn't want it to be perceived by my friends that I was not smart enough to go away to college. We probably were all feeling that way. Everyone was talking about where they were going to go. I didn't want to have to say I was going to our community college in our little town. I probably should have. More of them may have been brave enough to say they were going also. The thought at that age among my peers was if you went to a Junior College before going to a university, it was because you needed to improve your grades in order to be accepted into the University.

You don't have to go to your community college for two years to get your Associates Degree unless you want it. If you take the core classes I mentioned above, they will transfer where some of your other classes may not. Find out from the school where you will continue your education to find out what will and will not transfer. If you do get your Associates Degree, it may help you get better jobs while you're going to get your Bachelors Degree.

There are so many more things I can advise you on about college, but this book isn't geared toward that. Read my book that should be available soon titled, IF I KNEW THEN WHAT I KNOW NOW: THE COLLEGE EDITION.

I do want to add if you want to be a millionaire, avoid getting decks of credit cards. Do work to pay your student loans off as you acquire them, or save to pay for your classes for the next year. Check to see how much your classes and housing will cost. You will be amazed to know you can make the money at your summer job. I cannot remember any of the stuff I bought with my summer job money.

If you're in a position where you cannot stay at home with your parents to get a job in your field of expertise after you graduate, save for the unknown. You will be able to get a job in the city where you choose to live. It may not be the job you want, but it will take care of business until you get the one you want.

Save your extra money to save for a condominium until you decide to buy a house. You can always get a roommate to live in your condo. Don't tell them you own it. You'll find they think they should live rent- free or come up with reasons why you should understand why they couldn't pay. I know it's ridiculous that you can't tell them, but it's amazing how people will think you can cover them because you own the place, when you have to cover your part of the mortgage too. Check the law on evictions in case you need it.

CHAPTER TWENTY-NINE

STARTING OVER

It helps sometimes to get a fresh start. You can put all the mistakes you've made behind you and try it again. It's a part of life. We all have had to start over with something. Don't feel embarrassed or like you have to commit suicide. It's not that bad. If you've learned anything, you'll get to do it bigger and better the second time around.

You may have had your home foreclosed. You can buy another home. In fact, this time you can follow the plan in this book and save the money to buy it instead of trying to get a mortgage. You don't want to get bogged down in a lot of debt anymore.

Maybe you're bankrupt. You're not alone. That's why such a thing exists. Some people need a fresh start.

You should set the barometer in your life. You should not have to feel you have to measure up to what others believe you should. Unless they're paying your bills, they have no say so in how you spend your money. You can listen to others because sometimes they know something you may not that may benefit you. In the end, the decision is yours. You have to live with it.

CHAPTER THIRTY

SELF-SABOTAGE

There are some people who will never think they will be able to follow this plan. They will think there is no sense in even trying. Most of these people will live paycheck to paycheck for the rest of their lives because they will do everything they can to make sure of it. They are not going to stop shopping. They are going to be late on their bills. They will use their credit cards without abandon. I made my confession of being a shopoholic. I have to pray for strength to not sabotage myself. There are some things I want and I believe I should have them now. It's not true. I haven't died or become ill because I wasn't able to get something I wanted.

This plan is simple, pay the folks you're borrowing money from by using your credit cards or payday loans or whatever their money. Save some of your hard-earned money for yourself. The trade off is wonderful.

CHAPTER THIRTY-ONE

OVERNIGHT STARDOM

We have learned that overnight stardom is an oxymoron. When you do finally get the big payday. Wow! It can be a BIG check and a lot of other BIG checks following fast. There are no complaints about this happening in anyone's life. I have some advice for you if you are a celebrity with newfound wealth, or one whose wealth seems to come and go.

Sometimes we make a huge amount of money and we think we can buy the world when we can't. How can you determine how much money you can spend and live comfortably? I've contemplated this question also in trying to determine my standard of living. What I have determined is this: when you receive any earned money, pay your taxes first. You can get an accountant to help with your taxes. Your accountant will be able to help you calculate your payment to the IRS. This is a must to avoid going to the iron pen.

You must pay your tithe. This is ten percent of your earnings, ten cents from every dollar, a dime. Don't forget your offering. I will also remind you that your tithe and offerings can be filed on your taxes to reduce your tax debt. It all works out to your benefit.

Next, you need to realistically evaluate what you have left over and try to estimate how much more you will have coming in, not what you think you will make. You should

have a contract that lets you know what you'll be paid.
Based on this amount, you can now determine how you can
afford to live. If you have made a million, you'll probably
have about seven hundred thousand approximately available
to spend after taxes. You cannot afford a mansion right now.
If you're in your twenties, you will probably be able to live
off of twenty-five thousand dollars a year by a middle class
salary. Yea, I know! It's not a whole lot of money to flash
around like a star. This means you will have to keep doing
whatever it was you were doing to get that first million
several more times.

Yes. You can get some new clothes and goodies. I would
advise you to get a house. It would be better to get a house
instead of a high-priced apartment or anything you're not
signing for ownership. It will have to be a modest home.
You can always upgrade to a bigger, better home later after
you have worked some more and paid the IRS. Pay for this
home in full with your name on the mortgage.

You can use more than the twenty-five thousand to buy a
home because this is an investment that will benefit you.
Plus, as long as you've paid the IRS, there's no reason
anyone should be able to take it away from you. Because a
house is the largest item you will need to buy in the scheme
of life, you can afford to spend maybe two hundred thousand
dollars. Pay it in full. You will have to pay house insurance
and property taxes so you will need to put money aside for
those payments. I would put aside at least two hundred
thousand. This will cover you for a long time. If you're in
an area where you need a car, I would get a nice automobile,
but you cannot afford a Lamborghini, Rolls Royce and the
like. If you get one of these automobiles, you probably
should carry a few pillows and blankets in the trunk because
you may have to live out of it eventually.

If you're thirty, forty, or fifty it's not much better, but it's not
like you're on the side of the road with an "I will work for"

sign. You will need to make more money before you quit any of your jobs. You can chance investing. You can parlay your other talents into making speaking engagements or party promotions. Whatever comes your way that's legal and as long as you pay the IRS, do it.

As you make additional money you can adjust your yearly income. Let's say, for each additional million you earn, this is a good way to calculate it. Take out at least two to three hundred thousand dollars for taxes. This will adjust depending on how many dependents you claim and other items you can itemize.

If you're in a band or collaborating with other people, remember that all monies coming in have to be split among all parties. What may seem like a big windfall may be a breeze. Your family may think you can take care of them and all of their "doctor's bills", but a million dollars doesn't go that far nowadays. You will barely have enough to take care of yourself if you don't want to get a regular nine to five. Consider this when you're trying to help everyone. You should help your parents if they need help. You cannot help everybody you know. You'll end up broke and all those you helped will be laughing at you because you were foolish enough to give them some money if you don't plan.

I know you're probably thinking it's so silly of me to think you will have money problems because you're making so much money. There are numerous celebrities who have made lots of money, yet they ended their lives destitute. Celebrity life is fleeting. No one stays on top forever.

CHAPTER THIRTY-TWO

LOTTO WINS

BIG MONEY, BIG MONEY BIG MONEY. There's nothing like it. It can be a blessing. Some people make it a curse. The blessing is the freedom having lots of money can allow because it increases your choices. A curse can be brought from money if you do not know how to spend it **WISELY.** If you do not spend little or BIG money wisely, it will make for a harder to live life than is necessary.

The difference between this chapter and the previous is you know the exact amount of money you have won. There are conditions set up on how this money will be distributed to you. In some winnings you can decide to get the lump sum amount of your winnings or choose to get yearly distributions. In some instances you can only get it distributed in yearly installments.

This is how you should look at spending BIG money. If you get your money in yearly installments, this money will be your salary plus any money you will earn if you decide to continue to work the job you already have. When you receive your annual payment, you have to remember to make sure you divvy the money to take care of your needs for the entire year. This means you have to place enough money into savings for twelve months of utilities, phone bills, food, etc. You need to have a budget outlined and stick to it or you'll have to get a job unless you have someone taking care of these things for you. Any extra money after your necessities, you can have a party or go shopping or whatever pleases you.

If you are taking the lump sum payment option, you have to consider your age and the amount of money you have. You should calculate how many years you have until you will have to retire. If you are twenty, you will have about fifty years to retire based on the new retirement age of seventy. You also will need to consider some time after you retire also. If you make smart choices early, you'll make that living easy.

So, if you have a million dollars and you're twenty and you're thinking you can retire, you will have to learn to live off of approximately twenty thousand dollars a year. You have to consider any taxes. Chances are you will see that you will need to increase your money making pass this option. Basically, I'm telling you if you think you're going to retire after receiving a million dollars, you can, but your expenses have to be minimal. You cannot go and buy a million dollar home and live a life of luxury. The reason you won't be able to is, the IRS takes theirs before you get yours. Literally, you will not be receiving a million dollars. Just thinking you have a lot of money will make you spend more. You'll be broke before you know it. This doesn't mean I wouldn't want that million. It means you may have to continue to work or arrange great investments. There are no guarantees of great investments.

Consult an accountant about ways to reduce your tax debt. One thing I can suggest to reduce your taxes is by paying your tithes and offering. Believe it or not it will work. This isn't the reason to tithe. It's a benefit of tithing and offering. Always give your tithe with a cheerful spirit.

Let's say you are twenty and you win a million and you buy a home. Let's say you get a two hundred thousand dollar home. The IRS will probably take approximately three hundred thousand dollars. You're left with five hundred thousand. That's still a lot of money. You'll have to pay property taxes if you buy a house. It would be wise to get insurance on your home, your car, and yourself. All of these items cost money in addition to some other unforeseen expenses that always manage to pop up.

You're going to want a nice car and some clothes. Hopefully that won't take a full one hundred thousand. You're still doing okay. If you operate your life as an average middle class person, you will take vacations yearly.

With approximately four hundred thousand dollars, you can place your money in interest generating accounts or investments. You will need to speak with an accountant or financial planner. I will not advise on these things.

What I will say is do what makes you comfortable. Think about your options before you give your money to anyone to handle. Take your money out of any accounts when you began to feel uncomfortable with any of them. There are financial experts who do not think you should put your money in your basic savings accounts because they do not produce a lot of interest. These accounts do not take your money either. If you are comfortable having your money in a basic savings account do that until you learn more about money and investing. This can be your project to give you something to do. Take classes or go to your library and read as much as you can. You can start moving your money around as your knowledge increases. I think you should keep some in a savings account regardless of how much you learn. You don't want to go broke and there are so many scams and schemes out there. People are always thinking of ways to get your money for nothing.

CHAPTER THIRTY-THREE

DEATH BENEFITS

Inherited money is the worst kind of money to receive for most people. There's only one way to receive it, and although you know in advance you will receive it, it doesn't bring joy.

Some people advise waiting six months before making any major decisions on spending this money. I suggest if you have a mortgage and you will stay in the house, pay it off. Either way, if you decide to sell you will not have lost anything by having paid it off. It's an investment. You will not loose.

The reason I suggest paying your mortgage and any other bills off as soon as you can is if you don't, there are vultures out there who will try to cipher this money out of you before you have a chance to finish mourning.

CHAPTER THIRTY-FOUR

IF YOU'RE ON WELFARE

If you're on welfare, the first thing you're going to have to do is change your mind. What I mean by this is you're going to have to change your way of thinking. There's no way around this. You're going to have to decide you want to live a different way then you have been. This means you will have to do some things if not everything differently than you have done them before.

To help you change your mind and your way of thinking, the government has many programs to help you. The first thing you should do is, try to get as much education as you can. This will help redirect your thinking. If you haven't graduated from high school, you should work on getting your GED. There are some people who are so innovative; they do not have a diploma of any sort and they do well financially. This is not a determiner of whether or not you will be successful. If you are one of these people you have to know what to do and act on it.

After you get a diploma, you can further your education by going to college. You can also chose to go to a trade school. These are avenues of success. The biggest avenue of success is hard work. If you're willing to work hard, you can be successful.

If you're thinking you cannot afford to go to school, you can. If you're eligible, the government has grants and there are loans for which you can apply. You will need to talk with the administrators at your school of choice.

The biggest problem you may encounter is people who may try to discourage you from accomplishing your goals. This is the secondary part of changing your mind. You have to be strong enough to see this through to the end. There are people who will tell you it will take too long to finish school. Time is going to pass either way. Why not let it pass and in the end you can be happy you did what you wanted to do instead of regretting that you didn't.

They may tell you you're not smart enough to go to school. There's plenty of help available in this world for you to get all of the knowledge you and anyone else wants. There are libraries full of books. There are remedial classes you can take on any subject. There's the Public Broadcasting System (PBS). They have classes to help. Information has endless sources. Employment offices have computer classes if you're computer illiterate.

You have no excuses not to begin to change your mind and your life. If you believe you will face controversy from family and friends, don't tell them what you're doing. Sometimes that's what you have to do in order to accomplish your goals.

If you have children, you may not be able to work and go to school at the same time. They did not ask to be here. They need some of your time. You can begin to teach them by your example what they can achieve. You can also learn together. Plus, in some situations if you work you will become ineligible for aid. This can put you back at square one. Wait until you finish, then apply for work.

CHAPTER THIRTY-FIVE

MONEY FOR RETIREMENT

The problem with saving money for retirement is there's no way of knowing when you will die or more positively, how long you will live. You kind of have to wing it when guessing. My advice to you would be to have all major purchases paid in full. This means all mortgages should be paid in full. The earlier you pay off your mortgage, the more money you can save for retirement. This is the main focus of this book.

You should buy a relatively new vehicle a few years before you retire so hopefully you won't have a lot of maintenance. It should be paid in full.

You should have enough money saved to pay your maintenance expenses for at least twenty years I guess. You can only guess. This means at some point you should have sacrificed and saved.

I do believe you should invest in your 401k at your job or get an IRA. I do believe the younger you set it up the more money it will acquire even if you don't contribute to it yearly versus if you start it older and contribute to it faithfully. The premise of this book is for you to have more money saved if you're a person who doesn't understand or want to invest.

I don't know what will happen if you are not prepared, but I do know it will work out. A lot of older people are continuing to work. Don't be embarrassed if you have to continue. It's said retirement kills more people than it has ever saved.

CHAPTER THIRTY-SIX

HOW I CREATED AND USED THE PLAN

It didn't all come to me at one time. There were several
things I did over time and found that they really worked to
my benefit. There were as many things I've done that I
shouldn't have.

I've met a lot of people in my life who have financial
problems. I've made some bad financial mistakes myself.
I've learned some of the lessons. Some took being repeated
a time or two or three. There's a lot I'm still learning. I'm
still making some mistakes. I still have will power problems
when it comes to shopping. I can't always make myself stop
with some things. I have to have it. I've tried telling myself
life could be better if I didn't buy certain things and it means
nothing to my mind. I let you know this because I
understand. I go through periods where I can save lots of
money. Then, there are times where I will spend too much.
We all experience this.

After you've had bills for a while, it seems like you've
always had them. You haven't though. While you were
living with your parents, you didn't have bills.

My bills started in college of course. I learned how to lie on
the credit card applications with the best of them. I would
never get outrageous bills. I thought my phone bill, which
was eight dollars one time, was tortuous. I graduated college
with two thousand dollars of debt minus student loans, which
is the average. Some of my friends didn't graduate because

they had so much debt. They believed they needed to quit school in order to pay it off. I made the typical mistakes any person at that age would make.

The beginning of my credit woes was while I was in college. I served in the Army National Guard. My unit was deplored in the Desert Storm/Shield conflict. We were told at one meeting to go and withdraw from school. In the next meeting, we were told not to withdraw. Of course if you withdraw from school, the bank wants it's money and they did not care where I was. I thought this was very inconsiderate because there are humans who work there and they knew what was going on. When I returned to school I had to fill out a lot of paperwork to get my loans deferred to get back in.

After I graduated, like everyone else, I worried about paying my student loans back. I stressed trying to find a job within six months of graduating because that was the time given to defer payments. I lived paycheck to paycheck just like everyone else I know does. When I did start making good money, I paid those credit cards off.

I started doing a cash-only system for a while, then for whatever stupid reason, I would get a credit card again. During this time, I didn't pay off my student loan early. I planned to, but didn't make any concrete plans. I did end up paying them off early because they kept calling and saying I was late. They would send letters and I knew I had sent payments. I finally grew tired of it and I checked the balance. It was so close to being paid off, I sent a final check in to get rid of what I considered to be irritating calls and letters. It worked for them and it worked for me.

There were times when I was late on bills. There were times when I was working so much, I would forget the due date or mismanage my time where I wouldn't have sent the payment in and I would be too tired to go to the location to make the payment. After you calculate how much money you throw away by having fees for late payments in addition to the interest they charge on credit cards, it's enough to make you pay on time. It was for me.

The real change was when I decided I wanted a house. I thought I had to have perfect credit in order to get approved for a mortgage. I did not have the financial advice the financial gurus are giving now. I cashed out my 401K so I could pay off all of my bills. I had bought a new car two years prior to deciding to buy my house. I used some of the money to pay off the balance on this car. I used the rest to pay off my credit card bills and yes; I bought a couple of pairs of shoes and some clothes.

The mistake I made when I bought my car was I financed it with the dealership. I should have financed it with my credit union. I knew better, I somehow forgot. I refinanced it with my credit union later, but I wasted too much money in the process.

By the time I decided to get a house, I had lived in the New York/New Jersey area for about four years. Then, I moved to the Atlanta area for about six months before moving back to sweet home Alabama. I had started looking for a home in Atlanta. I got plenty of bad advice from agents over the phone. I didn't understand anything about buying a home. I was told I needed to get a pre-approval from the bank. I was skeptical about this because I know I didn't have a lot of debt at the time, but I knew I had some late payments on my record. I knew when I had left college I had a deck of credit cards. The good thing about it was I had no debt on most of the cards. Most of them were expired because I hadn't used them for years. I didn't know if this would hurt me or not.

As soon as I moved back to Alabama, I began looking for my home. I always wanted to live in a townhouse and that's what I found within the first week. I was still nervous about what the bank would say so I got a second job to try to help my chances because I was advised this would help. Then, I was told you would need to have the second job two years for it to be considered. Why didn't they tell me that in the beginning? Probably because I still hadn't gone to the bank. I quit that job immediately.

I went to the bank to get pre-approved. I had been avoiding the inevitable. I would go see how much damage I had done. In the end, I never found out how much I was pre-approved. I found a real estate agent who was new to the job. Neither of us probably knew what we were doing. She took me to look for homes with my specifications. I went into the bank with the information for the home I wanted and on November 19,1999 I moved into my home.

I didn't ask them the amount I was approved. They didn't tell me. I moved into my new dwelling. It's been prayed for and over for a safe and happy dwelling.

There was somebody who had the same name as mine who supposedly had bad credit. That's one reason we have social security numbers. Because of all of that stress, I decided I was going to make sure I paid everything on time forever. I decided I would save and pay for everything in cash. By the time I got the house, I was debt-free. I thought maybe I shouldn't get it for a second because I was totally debt-free. Oh well, I would have to pay to live somewhere so I moved in.

I was determined to not increase my debt load to decorate my house. I actually fulfilled this agreement I made with myself. Slowly, but surely month after month I decorated each room. I paid for each item with cash. My parents gave me some good gifts.

The one room I used a different approach with was the living room. I used the six-month no interest same as cash plan. I divided the total by five months and paid that amount each month. I paid the balance off early. I calculated it by five months instead of six because I didn't want to chance something happening and that last payment being late causing me to have to pay the interest. It saved me approximately a thousand dollars in interest by paying it that way.

The other thing that inspired me to get rid of debt and watch my money was the bank I had mortgaged my loan. They sent paperwork saying I could do automatic deductions and suggested if I wanted to pay my mortgage off sooner, I could send in one extra payment a year. By doing this it would eliminate some of the interest. If I were to pay my mortgage as dictated in my contract, I would end up paying approximately two hundred thousand dollars in interest. What?!

I knew I had to do something about that. The automatic deductions by the bank would be an extra five dollars a month. Please! I could pay it myself and save that five dollars a month. All of this helped me devise a plan. I see so many places where companies are trying to take a few dollars here and there. I started paying my auto insurance six months at a time to avoid paying the five dollars they charge you for paying your insurance monthly.

I have been debt free and will for some crazy reason get into debt again. Sometimes it will be to save fifteen percent on an outfit. I will learn.

My goal now is to become debt free and not get into the trap again. I could have had my house paid off by now. I did not realize that it was possible.

When I got my house, I had about fifteen hundred dollars a month for my leisure after bills. If I had put that toward my mortgage, I could have paid my house off in six years. I didn't need a lot of clothes because my job didn't have a dress code and I didn't wear the clothes I was buying there anyway.

Another motivation for the plan was I wanted to upgrade my car and buy a Jaguar. In considering the price of this automobile I thought it's about like driving around in a house. I would have to finance this purchase. The payment would have been more than my mortgage. The amazing thing is I could finance it, and pay it off in a shorter amount of time than I was paying my mortgage. Who decided a mortgage had to be paid off in fifteen or thirty years? Is there any reason we can't pay them off in say five or ten years? If you do, with the interest you'll save you'll avoid paying for a second home you'll never get to live in.

I'm working from home now because I want to be able to have a more hands on approach in raising my little princess. I'm thinking about life and I pull out my old income tax information, old check stubs, and paper. I calculate how close to a million dollars I've made in my life. I only calculated since my husband and I have been married. I didn't calculate what either of us made before we got married. We're both over thirty.

I was amazed at the amount. We do not have what I would have imagined I would if I had received all that at one time. I thought about how could we have maximized our spending so we could take more advantages with our money in the future. I examined my old check stubs and realized if we had spent our money differently we could have paid our mortgage off. It was more my fault than his. He paid the mortgage. I had suggested we both pay a full mortgage payment instead of splitting it in half like roommates. We both had good jobs. If we had done like I suggested, we would have paid our mortgage off in less than six years.

Life happened and I became unfocused. I was transferred to another location and wasn't making as much money. Then, I got sick. In that time I did pay all of my credit card and student loan debt off.

An opportunity came up to own a business. I started not to take it because I didn't have any debt again. It was such a great opportunity. I said I would not get in deep debt so I took out loans to start the business. Yes, I did it again. I told myself I would pay all of the loans off with the money earned from the business each month. I made enough where I could pay all of the loans off in a year. This is what I had projected I would do and I could have done it. The problem: I was not making the money yet that I had been making at my job yet, but I continued to spend in my personal life like I was. Plus, I got sick again. Health insurance covered my medical bills, but I had used some of the money from the loans for personal purchases instead of paying the loans as I had projected. I had not been in business long enough to establish it so it could run without me being present. I'm in debt again. It will be paid off because I always pay my debt off eventually.

I have to ask myself what I will do differently so I don't get caught in the debt cycle again. This is what I've determined that can help you and me. If I were to pay my mortgage off and any other debt (credit cards and loans), I will save for any future purchases. I would save even if I didn't have a future purchase in mind. If I wanted to start a business, I would save the rent to cover the entire contract obligation. I will save so I can experience having a million dollars. The reason a millionaire is a millionaire is not because they spend all of their money. They are millionaires because they have it available to spend, but they save it. And they do not carry interest around to eat up their money.

CHAPTER THIRTY-SEVEN

DOUBTS ABOUT THE PLAN

If you're thinking what are the chances of anyone doing any of this. Why not? You'll sacrifice wasting money on a lot of toys you're really never getting to play with anyway. Besides sacrificing for a few years compared to most of your life is a fair trade off.

Do you realize how great your life will be debt free? You won't have to work overtime or get a second job. You can change jobs and work doing what you enjoy. You can have money saved to pay for your vacations in advance of going. You will get to truly relax since you don't have any debt. Life doesn't get any better than this. You'll start seeing yourself becoming a millionaire since you're going to be saving your money. Imagine saving twenty thousand dollars or more a year. This is the good life.

Even if you do not care to be a millionaire because you're thinking more money causes more problems. If you follow the basic elements of this plan, you can have a happier more stress-free life. If more marriages end because of financial problems, imagine how many marriages could possibly survive.

I did some research about debt. One of the oldest resources I found information was the Bible. Of course it speaks of tithing. What it discussed on debt was everyone was to pay off debt and be forgiven for any debt they had every seven years. The reason for this it states was so there would be no poverty. Perhaps this is the reason bankruptcy last for seven years?

I have shown you several examples of how you can accomplish this. These were the instructions God gave to Israel upon their entrance into the Promised Land. I wonder will we do as they did and get punished for forty years for what could have been a three-day trip for not living our best lives.

Will you pay your mortgage in thirty years or three to six years? Will you carry debt until death do you part or will you pay it off in seven years or less? The choice is yours to make.

CHAPTER THIRTY-EIGHT

MY CONCLUSION

Hopefully this information has helped you make some great financial changes. It has helped me too. I cannot believe I had the ability to write this book because I have made so many financial mistakes.

After some thought about the subject matter, I realized, why not me. I have made a lot of financial mistakes because of small things I did not know about money. I have avoided some mistakes because I have listened to and followed some of the advice my family and teachers have given. I will not berate myself for not having avoided the mistakes I have made. I pledge right here and now I will do better. I am going to take those clothes back that I know I am not going to wear. I will evaluate my purchases of toys I like to buy. I do not need to buy any more until I use the ones I have already purchased. Yes, that's my pledge.

I'm publishing this book because of this: If I know there is a hole in the road in front of you, I will feel guilty if I do not warn you of the hole. If you fall in the hole after I've told you the hole was up ahead, it is not my fault you fell in. I do not like giving advice for the point of being right and having you think I'm going to say I told you so. When I give advice, I give it in the spirit of making your life easier to live. What I've learned in life is, what may work for me may not work for you.

I hope when you try at least one part of my plan it works to your benefit. Do not condemn it without trying at least one part of it.

Thank you very much for reading my book. I hope it was well written, cohesive, and informative.

THE END

ORDER THIS BOOK AT

AMAZON.COM

TO CONTACT KATHRYN M. CRAIG

WITH QUESTIONS OR COMMENTS

WILLCH@BELLSOUTH.NET